# From the **BACK** of the **PEWS**

# To the **HEAD** of the **CLASS**

## The Remarkable Accomplishments
## of a Segregated Catholic High School
## in the Deep South

• • • • •

Compiled and Organized
with Introductions by Robert McClory

*acta*
PUBLICATIONS

FROM THE BACK OF THE PEWS TO THE HEAD OF THE CLASS
The Remarkable Accomplishments
of a Segregated Catholic High School in the Deep South

Compiled and organized with introductions by Robert McClory

Cover and text design by Patricia A. Lynch

Photo on page 16 submitted by Mrs. Larleitta Hall.

Photo on page 124 courtesy of the Palmer Studio Collection, The Doy Leale McCall Rare Book and Manuscript Library, University of South Alabama. Used with permission.

Copyright © 2013 National Center for the Laity

Published by ACTA Publications, 4848 N. Clark Street, Chicago, IL 60640, (800) 397-2282, www.actapublications.com

Library of Congress Catalogue Number: 2013941917
ISBN: 978-0-87946-510-0
Printed in the United States of America by Total Printing Systems
Year 25 24 23 22 21 20 19 18 17 16 15 14 13
Printing 20 19 18 17 16 15 14 13 12 11 10 9 8 7 6 5 4 3 2 First

# Contents

## DEDICATION

*This book is dedicated to all of the students of Most Pure Heart of Mary High School, the Franciscan Sisters of Philadelphia, the Sisters of the Holy Spirit of San Antonio, the Dominican Sisters of Sinsinawa, and the Josephite Fathers.*

• • • • •

All profits from the sale of this book will go to the education of African American students, with priority to the Tuition Assistance Fund for students who attend most Pure Heart of Mary Elementary School. If Most Pure Heart of Mary Elementary School should ever close, these profits will be used for tuition assistance for African American students of other Sinsinawa Dominican schools.

*Alexis Herman*

# Foreword

......................................................................................................

*"The kingdom of Heaven is like a mustard seed which indeed is the least of all seeds, but when it is grown, it is the greatest among the herbs and becomes a tree." Matthew 13:31*

......................................................................................................

During a weekend retreat in the mountains of Virginia, outside Washington, D.C., Sister Patricia (Alberta) Caraher OP, Sister Marilyn (Antonietta) Aiello OP, Paulette Norvel Lewis and I reminisced about our days at Most Pure Heart of Mary High School. We marveled at the radical faith, revolutionary hope and bold action reflected in the Heart of Mary experiences. We also recounted the continued sense of community and ongoing commitment to service among its alumni. It occurred to us that these stories contained valuable lessons that should be documented for those who work to educate future generations and for those who struggle to overcome social and cultural barriers.

We commissioned a series of interviews with former students and others (short biographies are included in chapter XV) and then asked Robert McClory, a well-respected Catholic author and journalist, to compile and organize this oral history and provide introductions throughout the book to put the reflections in historical context. We thank him for his dedication and skill in bringing this book to fruition.

*From the Back of the Pews to the Front of the Class* documents the moving and sometimes dramatic stories of students, teachers and priests who witnessed to Christianity during a period which reflected some of the most revolutionary social changes in the history of the United States and the Catholic Church. The authors lived through and benefited from the remarkable workings of the Spirit in a small black Catholic high school in Mobile, Alabama. Most Pure Heart of Mary High School was the only Catholic high school available to black children in southern Alabama and Mississippi from the early 1940s to the end of the 1960s.

Though the students were segregated with inferior resources, they were rich in talent, in community and in the gifts of the Spirit. Like the tiny mustard seed, they were considered by law and treated by local customs as "the least of these." Despite the odds and with the support and commitment of their teachers and the love and faith of their families and community, many Heart of Mary students rose to unimaginable heights. Many have gone on to become leaders in business, government, medicine, education, church, the military, the arts, and politics. They continue to lead compelling and courageous lives as they work to bring about the "Beloved Community."

The story of HOM graduate William Kelly leaves you with an indelible mental picture of a little boy sitting on the lap of a courageous white nun who refused to move to the back of the bus. Dora Finley tells the story of a fear-gripping moment when she was first called a "nigger"—a "nigger" accused of stealing a fallen pecan from a sidewalk at the age of eight! She thought all white people were the same, until caring teachers at Heart of Mary changed that perception forever. There are of course many fun-loving episodes such as Paulette Norvel Lewis' story, in which she reminds us of some of the disguises we had to assume in order to survive. In this instance, a group of Heart of Mary girls had to pretend to be international students just so they could be served milkshakes and hamburgers at the local Dairy Queen.

My own story is about disguising my intent to confront the bishop by requesting to kiss his ring. This was my first lesson in what it means to take risks to stand up for what is right. It led to my being expelled from Heart of Mary. It was also my first lesson in what it means to be supported by people who loved and believed in me. But whether it is mine, William Kelly's, Dora Finley's or Paulette Norvel Lewis' story, the message is the same: if we expect great things from our children, we will get them, no matter the circumstances.

It is important to note that the students represented in this book are just the tip of a very large iceberg. They are by no means meant to represent the "best and the brightest." There are many, many more stories just as interesting and intriguing. You can be sure, however, that wherever you find Heart of Mary alumni, they will be working to serve the community and/or the church. They are like the grown up seeds in the parable—tall trees.

Many will ask why we produced this book and what these experiences might teach us in our present political and racial environment. In our fast paced global society with so many distractions—from gun violence in our schools, to fractured families, to the impact of Facebook and Twitter—all of which can lessen a sense of community, we could ask ourselves if these stories are relevant today. I respond with a resounding "Yes." Times change, but values don't. Even in the midst of these changing times, we must still challenge ourselves as a nation and in our different communities to pass on our stories and our values. As Marion Lewis, a Heart of Mary graduate and former Wendy's executive, says in his story, much of what we learned is still applicable today. "Parents must be still involved; there is a lot to be said for structure and using structure positively and not letting kids figure it out on their own. There is still a need for discipline, properly applied…."

Like my mother and father before me, I am honored and blessed to be part of the incredible legacy of faith, service, community, learning, leadership and love that is Most Pure Heart of Mary High School. It will always be an empowering source of strength for me and for almost everyone who crossed its threshold as student or teacher. And, like the prophet Zachariah, I remain a "prisoner of hope" for the future, for our children, and for our schools—inspired even more by the stories in this book.

............................................................................................................

**THE HONORABLE ALEXIS HERMAN**, *a graduate of Heart of Mary High School, was U.S. Secretary of Labor under President Bill Clinton.*

............................................................................................................

*Dora Finley*

# I. Remembering Dora Finley

*It's less than two miles from the majestic Cathedral Basilica of the Immaculate Conception in downtown Mobile, Alabama to the humble Most Pure Heart of Mary church and school in what was once the city's historic black ghetto. The cathedral stands proudly amid quality hotels, good restaurants and shops, while the Heart of Mary complex sits amid vast, vacant, unpopulated stretches of grass, weeds and a few lonely trees; the closest signs of urban life are some low slung factories and industrial buildings in the distance.*

*On a very warm Saturday afternoon in mid-June, 2012, the cathedral was the setting for the funeral of Dora Finley, one of Mobile's best known and most active black citizens. She lived most of her life in this city until she was struck down too soon by cancer at the age of 59. I'm sure Dora would have preferred to have the service at Heart of Mary, but that was not an option, given the crowds expected by the funeral planners. They were not mistaken.*

*People came from all directions, mostly African-Americans but with a substantial representation of whites and people of other races. Despite the warmth, many of the men wore crisp, three-piece suits with ties, while many women were in formal dresses, more than a few wearing the wide brimmed colorful hats reserved for very special occasions. For an hour before the service, the Excelsior band, a staple in Mobile since 1883, played subdued Dixieland selections just outside the cathedral's main doors as a seemingly endless procession of the public entered the church and slowly made their way up a side aisle to the front to pay their last respects to the deceased and to offer sympathy to Dora's daughter, mother and a flock of other relatives near the altar.*

*There was a certain irony in this long line of mostly black folks wending their way up the aisle, some chatting in hushed tones with friends and neighbors as they went. For most of its history this Cathedral of the Immaculate Conception was off limits to blacks and mixed-blood worshippers, except for two or three pews in the far back on one side of the church, where a few might be begrudgingly accommodated. And when the procession of clergy finally marched up the center aisle* and the Mass began, there was a touch of irony too in the presence of Mobile Archbishop Thomas Rodi, who would preside at this funeral liturgy, with retired Mobile Archbishop Oscar Lipscomb concelebrating and a representation of other Mobile priests present in the sanctuary. For decades, including the time Dora Finley and her generation were growing up, few human beings were more resented and distrusted in the black Catholic community than Thomas Toolen, then the archbishop of Mobile. Civil segregation they could understand and live with. But few blacks could comprehend how the message of Jesus required the separation of races in Catholic churches and schools. Fewer still could understand why on the great public celebrations of Catholicism every year, when all the city's Catholic high schools marched through the streets of Mobile, Heart of Mary students had to come last.

Dora Finley had attained respectability and recognition from both church and state. The Mobile City Council issued a proclamation praising her and her achievements. The Mobile Press-Register called her a "tireless leader," an outstanding "advocate for historic restoration," a "diplomat and organizer, who leaves behind a legacy that will not be soon forgotten." She was a member of a family with deep roots in Mobile. Her grandfather, the first black to graduate from University of Michigan Medical School, served the Mobile community for more than 50 years. Mobile's Franklin Clinics are named in his honor. Dora's father, a pharmacist, and her mother, a teacher, were active, along with their children, in Mobile's civil rights movement. They took part in an historic Mobile march and were arrested.

Dora herself never stopped marching. After earning a degree from Eastern Michigan University, she had a 25-year career as manager of logistics for the Scott Paper Co./ Kimberly Clark Corp. headquartered in Mobile. She became active in civic and religious enterprises, serving as a board member on numerous community foundations and organizations including the Alabama Trust for Historic Preservation, the Jewish and Christian Dialogue and the Historic Mobile Preservation Society. She also served as president of the Mobile Historic Development Commission and as chair of the African-American Heritage Trail. In recent years the trail had been her major passion. Scotty Kirkland, an editorial board member of the Press-Register, called her "the driving force" behind the project. "Through countless presentations, phone calls and just the right amount of arm-twisting," he wrote, "she built around her a coterie of supporters and launched the trail, which today has placed more than 40 markers throughout Mobile County commemorating historic African-American people, places and events."

Several times during her well rehearsed tour narratives, she would gently remind the participants of the simple but profound theme behind the trail: "You can't know where you're going until you know where you've been." In a sense that is what this book is all about.

Given her active life, you might be tempted to regard Dora Finley as one of these rare, amazing persons who use their time and talents to the maximum, people whose lives make a real contribution to the world, and a contributor she surely was, but her life was not as rare as it might seem at first glance. This book records the words of many former Heart of Mary students, including Dora, who were interviewed about their experiences. Their words place a kind of magnifying glass on this community and on this school at a critical time in its history and raise important questions about education that still reverberate in our own time. An intriguing, underlying question is, how can one explain the fact that so many students who came from this small, secluded, segregated, under-funded institution emerged with the capability and determination to function as achievers and equals in an officially desegregated world? Now, more than 50 years later, we know how well many did succeed, not just for themselves but often with a desire to give back, as Dora Finley believed, to those who would come after.

Dora's stories about her education are similar in many ways to those of fellow students at Heart of Mary. It's clear that many factors worked together to create a kind of special aura around the school, not just in the 1960s (the years when most of the interviewees attended) but in its earlier years as well.

Here are a few excerpts from her interview, which she provided in late 2010, about 18 months before her death. They give a hint of the dynamics still at work in this special place—until the high school held its last graduation in 1968.

Now here you had a little school that didn't have all the tools and material and facilities, but from it came some of the great minds and contributors to the African-American community. And it helped to develop among us a consciousness of righteousness. That may sound corny, but for this group of people it provided a foundation....

When you started you were in the same class each year with the same people. So after first grade you went with the same students into second grade. After a while you spent more time with them than you spent at home. And these children that you grew up with in those classes, they became like your brothers and your sisters. You got to know them and you made relationships and were close to them. And as you know, those relationships can be endearing in their honesty. And that place you are living in then, you can never replicate that as you get older....

The nuns encouraged us to be free thinkers, to be independent thinkers. They didn't just talk the talk, they walked the walk. In classroom activities we had stimulating conversation all the time, and there was never a feeling that you were inhibited, that you could say the wrong thing or give the wrong answer. And they wouldn't allow anyone to disrespect what someone else was saying. It helped the environment we had, you know, those ties we had developed in being children together. So we already had a bond and the ability to respect one another. And we bought into their way of thinking, because these women were so well versed in being open and pulling us out of our isolation. They were great facilitators. So when I came along it was a special time in our development as African-Americans, as black people.

I'm proud of my family, those that came before me and those that are coming after. I'm proud of my parents and grandparents and the rich heritage and legacy they provided. I'm proud of my youngest brother who was nine years old when my father died, and he is now an attorney who fights for justice. I'm proud of my sister who produces great minds, particularly in the area of business at Florida A & M University. I'm proud of my oldest brother, whose company manufactures parts for the automobile industry. And I'm proud of my daughter, who has her Ph.D. in molecular and cellular biology and is working to make a difference in the world, to make it a better place. And I'm proud of the heritage trail I'm working on: to research, bring out the past and make it present to young minds today. When both white and black come to respect each other and each other's contributions, we will have a stronger foundation to propel the next generation into the future. This is what happened to me and helped me to be active, because I come from a strong people who have come all the way from slavery to the things the people in my own family have been able to accomplish.

*Heart of Mary High School*

*Heart of Mary High School Graduating Class, 1944*

# II. A Solid Cornerstone: The Earlier Years

*Most Pure Heart of Mary was founded in 1898 as a parish for black Catholics, under the direction of priests of the Josephite order. Plans were made for the construction of a school, and thanks to a donation from Sister Katherine Drexel (later declared a saint by the Catholic Church), a grammar school opened in 1902, staffed by two Franciscan Sisters of Philadelphia, with an enrollment of 59 students. The sisters left in 1907, and for four years parents and other laity kept the growing school afloat. In 1911 the Holy Ghost Sisters of San Antonio took over at Heart of Mary and taught there for 31 years, adding a complete high school curriculum in 1917. They departed in 1942 and were replaced in 1943 by the Dominican Sisters of Sinsinawa, Wisconsin, who provided staff for 31 years, until 1989. The laity returned to staff the Heart of Mary Grammar School until 1993 when the Philadelphia Franciscan sisters came back.*

*This sheer survival of the school amid a maze of changes and adjustments testifies to the determination of the Heart of Mary community. The people placed great value in the presence of the grammar school and extraordinary value in the high school—the only black Catholic high school within 150 miles of Mobile during its 51 years of existence. For much of the 20th century the city had three other Catholic high schools: McGill Institute for Boys, Toolen High School for Girls and the Convent of Mercy High School, also for girls. The three accepted white students only. With the coming of integration in 1968, HOM and the Convent of Mercy High School closed. McGill and Toolen continued operation, merging in 1972, but its enrollment has remained predominantly white.*

*It was in the 1960s that the high school achieved some of its proudest moments and faced its hardest challenges. But even in the earlier days an unmistakable sense of pride was evident. In this chapter older alumni speak out. Well past their 70th year, some in their 90s, their recall of details is amazing, and the one thing the words "Heart of Mary" seems to call to their minds is delight.*

***William Kelly***, *who became a teacher and coach,*
*was born in the late 1930s.*

We had our own close-knit community and didn't go out of the community too often without adults and certainly for the most part only in daylight. And the beauty of that was Heart of Mary was located on what we called the main drag, which was Davis Avenue. *[Named in honor of Jefferson Davis!]*

One person I remember from school was Sister Ronald (Thibodeau). This woman was beautiful, as many of the sisters were; don't get me wrong. Well, they had a vocation day once a year for seniors. It was held at McGill Institute, and all the Catholic schools would send their seniors. Of course, we were the only black Catholic high school. And we got along fine at recess playing softball with the fellows from McGill, and they got ready to go to lunch. Sister Ronald, our principal, bless her heart, puts us in line and says, "C'mon gang, let's get ready to go eat." And this brother comes out, a brother of the Sacred Heart, with a big cross on him, and says, "Sister, I'm afraid these children can't eat until the white kids finish." And these were Sister Ronald's words: "Brother, I'll be damned if that's so!" She said, "C'mon gang, let's go home." And Lord have mercy, we did; we just walked off. That woman was a hero. Can't you see how that kind of thing gives children hope?

Oh man, these priests and nuns, for the most part they lived the crucifixion with us in our community. I got on the bus one day when I was still pretty little to pay the rent downtown. When I was coming back the bus was packed. And there sitting in the front seat were two of my teachers, two nuns. All the colored people had to sit behind a certain section. So as I got on, sister grabbed me, picked me up and put me on her knee. The bus driver says, "Sister, that boy can't sit with you." She says, "I don't see why not. I teach him every day in school." And that's where I stayed. For the whole ride. Oh man, imagine what that does for a child!

I started at Heart of Mary in 1943, in kindergarten, and a lot of us are still in contact to this day. All those boys and girls, well, they're all old men and women now. And we often say as we got older that we didn't know how much we loved one another. "This is my commandment that you love one another." Heart of Mary was a commandment-keeping place. At that time we had a poverty situation that was unbelievable. It really was. And there we were at Mass signing Gregorian chant and praying in Latin. And today, God bless us, we can hardly pronounce English.

One of the memories that sticks out is when I started playing football, I got a little cute and decided to slack off on studies, especially math. I could do math, but I didn't study for a test and I did very, very poorly. In fact, I failed it. And I'm out there, just got out of the shower house at the football field ready for practice. And Sister Ronald, who taught math by the way, comes along and says, "William Kelly, you need to go to the shower house, change clothes and come over to the convent. We need to go over that test." The coach comes over and says, "Sister, uh, we've got a big game on Friday." She says, "William's education is more important than any football game." He says, "Sister, I'm the head coach." And she says, "I'm the principal!" I get up, go to the shower house and change clothes. And the embarrassment that I brought on myself really drove home a message to me, you know? And when I became a coach later, I carried it on to my students every time it was necessary. She showed me and I thank her for it.

........................................................................................

*Jacqueline Rice was 91 years old when this interview was conducted. She has lived in Mobile most of her life.*

........................................................................................

I graduated in 1941. We had a class of 32 members. I counted this morning and we have eight living. We had the Holy Ghost sisters then, and the priest was Father (Vincent) Warren (SSJ), which was lovely. Back then it was hard for our parents. Tuition wasn't but a dollar a month, but it was still hard. My family was determined that I was going to go to Heart of Mary. In fact, my aunt graduated from there in 1929, so the tradition was going on.

*Jacqueline Rice*

But I started out at St. Peter Claver School. That was my foundation. All of us who lived in the Down the Bay area south of town would meet up every day at a certain destination, and we'd all carry our lunch since we didn't have a cafeteria then. We'd walk straight up Dearborn Street, and we were so glad when we got to that little cement step, to step on it and go into school. All the children would line up outside, and I would play the piano for the children to march in. And when it was time for school to let out, I'd ring the bell. Sister would look over at me and say, "Go ring the bell please, Jacqueline." I would be so glad because that meant Latin class was over. I would tell my friend, Donald Sylvester, who sat in front of me, bless his heart. I would punch him in the back and I would say, "Oh, saved by the bell." And sister would say, "Jacqueline, please ring the bell!" *[She laughs.]*

I remember when I got to Heart of Mary, they had the most wonderful stage with a beautiful green velvet curtain. We used to have plays and skits and a glee club. Father Warren used to love to come over and hear us sing "Somewhere Over the Rainbow" and "My Old Kentucky Home." Well, when we were practicing, something funny would come up, and we'd start laughing. Sister would say, "Everybody, stop laughing!" And I couldn't stop myself sometimes. They said I had an infectious laugh. So we'd all end up laughing, even if some of the class didn't know what we were laughing about.

*For many years Mobile had two Mardi Gras, one for whites, one for colored.*

For the Mardi Gras in our senior year I was selected to be the queen for Heart of Mary. I knew I wasn't able to put up the money, but everybody worked like Trojans to raise money and they did it. So I got to sit up high on the float. I was so happy and excited just riding on that float with people cheering and hollering. And when the float got around to Heart of Mary...oh, that did it! Our people were out there in droves!

I especially remember graduation because we were going to the cathedral, the first class that finished at the cathedral. I could hardly wait to get that cap and gown on. And on Holy Thursday, we'd go to church early in the morning, and we'd get to strew flowers in the church. After Mass we'd go home, get our breakfast and start out visiting the Catholic churches. That was the custom then. And our group from Down the Bay, we made all the churches in town, every one of them, on Holy Thursday. I'm so glad I got my Catholic education. It meant so much to me and still does.

**Elaine Palmer**, *a classmate and lifelong friend of Jacqueline Rice, raised nine children. She has also lived most of her life in Mobile.*

To me, Heart of Mary was like a shining star. I loved being there. I always felt so safe. Nothing bad ever happened to me or to anybody else, really. Times were so much better than they are now. I pity these poor children today, how they have so much more to put up with that we never had.

Besides teaching us our religion, reading, writing and arithmetic, the nuns taught us practical things. I learned how to patch up the books. When the school year was out, we had to patch the books and put them away for the summer. And when September came we could go get the books out again and put them back in the classroom where they belonged. I was always in dances and choir and glee club. So I give the Heart of Mary nuns a lot of credit. I think they were responsible for my love of dance and music. I used to play the pipe organ for two Masses on Sunday. Those sisters devoted a lot of time to us. And they demanded that we respond the same way. There was no such thing as goofing off, you know?

After high school I went to Alabama A&M for just one year. I got married in 1946 and we moved to New York. I didn't like it. I didn't like the cold. I came back to Mobile, and I never did go back to New York. I had nine children, five girls, four boys, and they all went to Heart of Mary at one time or another. So when the high school closed, some had to go to Toolen or McGill.

Looking back, I think I raised a fairly wonderful family—nothing spectacular but they're very caring. If one of us is in trouble, they'll all stop what they're doing and take off from work and stay with that one while they're sick. And that's the kind of children they are. And that was what I always wanted. They're wonderful, wonderful to me. What little bit I had, it had to be spread around so many. My children think I did a lot. I really didn't do that much."

..................................................................................................

*Larleitta Hall talks of the difference between the Holy Ghost sisters and the Dominican nuns and how all the girls learned the Irish jig and other unusual dances.*

..................................................................................................

From first grade all the way through eleventh we had the Holy Ghost sisters at Heart of Mary. Then the Dominicans came in 1943, so I had only one year with them. I graduated in 1944. We were always curious about how the nuns lived, always going around in pairs. And they wore these habits. Living in Mobile all my life, I know the climate is warm and humid most of the time. And with all that on, I just wondered how they could stand it. But anyway, they never seemed to perspire or be uncomfortable. Never! And they had this, you know, thing around their face. You never saw hair or anything, just the face.

The Holy Ghost nuns were extremely strict. We were like little soldiers. When you came out of the classroom you line up. When you went back to the classroom you were lined up. When we went to church we were lined up. When we went into the pews you were lined up. And you were always marching. It was really militaristic. But the Dominican sisters were more human, more like ordinary people. At the end of the school year we had a festival, and every grade had to perform. The Holy Ghost nuns taught us Irish jigs and dances. The nuns I remember at that time were Irish, and they showed us what to do. The nuns got pictures of Irish dancing costumes, and my mother sewed them. I knew nothing about Ireland. I think they thought it was more, uh, cultural than other kinds of dances.

For school we always wore uniforms. In warm weather it was an all over white dress with a ribbon tie. In the winter it was a blue serge uniform with a white collar and cuffs. We wore white socks, what they used to call hosettes then; they came up to your knee. And everything had to be clean. You couldn't wear anything dirty. *[She laughs.]*

And they could tell if you messed up, you know. They had a little stick, not really a switch. And if you got out of line, they tapped you to begin with. And if you kept getting out of line, they'd pull you aside and say, "Put out your hands." Bam, bam, bam!

*[She raps on the table for emphasis.]* Actually, they didn't hit too hard. I never got it too hard. I would get it for talking—running off at the mouth. During Lent they would haul you off to church every Thursday and Friday, I think. You had your first through eighth grades on one side of the church and nine through twelfth on the other side. And each teacher sat with her grade. So you did not mess up because sister was right there. During Lent there was a Wednesday night service and Stations of the Cross on Fridays.

When the Dominicans came for my senior year, we put on a whole operetta, *Sunbonnet Sue*. We were so good the nuns had us perform over at Toolen. Well, I had a song to sing myself, and I was so afraid I'd forget parts of the song. And I did. On the stage, the words would not come to me. So I hummed and made up words and went "tra la la la la." I gave my own version of the song. Sister asked, "What happened?" I told her I forgot the words. But nobody else knew because they thought what I did was part of the song.

We had a retreat my senior year with Father Vincent Warren. He had built a church and school across the bay for small towns over there. But he was pastor at Heart of Mary when the Dominicans came. He was a man ahead of his time. He brought black Catholics and Baptists and Methodists together. He invited them to his church and he went to theirs. It wasn't anything for him to give a sermon in these other churches. That was something unheard of at that time. Everybody just loved him. He was really a man for all seasons.

I've tried to be a very good Catholic. I think that's the legacy that Heart of Mary passed on: to be a good student and a good Catholic. That means you lived by the Ten Commandments, and you didn't get into trouble, and you didn't go to jail. You were a good neighbor, you were honest and you tried to live right. All those years of segregation, I just accepted it, and I felt that's the way it was. It's the funniest thing though. Now when I'm older, it makes me angry. Segregation was wrong. And I try not to get angry about it because it's over. I shouldn't make myself angry about something that happened years ago. I might run my pressure up! I have to think about my health now. I'm 84 years old.

......................................................................................................

*Sister Genevieve of St. Teresa OCD (Genevieve Sogata) graduated from Heart of Mary in 1950. Six months after graduation, she entered the Carmel monastery in Mobile, became a Carmelite sister, and remained there for more than 50 years.*

......................................................................................................

After my first day at Pure Heart of Mary I went home and I said, "Mom, I don't want to go back to high school. They give too much homework." In grade school we studied in school more, and the teachers gave us very personal help. And when we got to Heart of Mary, we got lots of homework and lots of books to take home. My mom said, "Let's try it for a few more days. Maybe you'll like it." And by the end of the week, I didn't even want to come home! The sisters were so wonderful.

I remember Sister Martin De Porres (Hogan) and Sister Eulogia (Dawes) and Sister Marie Eugene (McBride), who taught us music and history. Of all the classes, I liked music best, and Latin was good too. Sister Marie Eugene had a good phonograph player, and she played the records of classical composers. She told us about the composer and we were to pay strict attention to the music and try to understand what his music was all about. Well, it was all news to us, because none of us had recordings at home. We had a very good band at school, and we traveled a lot, playing at football games, at parades and Mardi Gras, and at the big ceremony for Christ the King. I played the soprano saxophone. I got into the school band when I was nine years old, and I wanted to play the trombone. The teacher did a little laugh and she said, "Your arms aren't long enough. I'm gonna suggest the saxophone, and I'm gonna get you a little one because you're too little for a big one. *[She laughs.]* That's how I got started.

*Sister Martin de Porres Hogan*

I always wanted to be a religious, from about the time I was in sixth grade. I knew it was a calling from God, but Pure Heart of Mary guided us, you know. The sisters guided us in our religion and faith, and most of us went to daily Mass. It was wonderful, grace just falling into our souls all the time. We were imbued with the love of the Blessed Sacrament and all the other devotions. It wasn't only an academic education. It was a pattern for life. The sisters introduced me to a sub-prioress of the Dominican order when she was down here one time. And I went to Chicago one summer and met the mother general, I think it was Sister Evelyn.

But I was reading a book about St. Teresa after an exam in high school, and there was a picture of her with the sacred Mass vessels.

She was preparing for Mass. And since I had been a sacristan at St. Peter Claver at that time, I thought that's one thing I can do. I didn't want to be a Dominican because you had to study all the time. *[She laughs.]* And so that's what really attracted me to Carmel. But the Lord played a trick on me. I never became a sacristan at Carmel. He wanted me to be a cook. So I had to learn to cook because I didn't know a thing about cooking. So I cooked in the Carmel monastery for over 50 years. I didn't really enjoy it. I did it for the love of God. As Carmelite nuns, we live lives of poverty and silence, of prayer, penance and sacrifice, hoping to make reparation for the losses and sufferings of the church and the ills of the world at large. Our scope then is the whole world, though the main work of the Carmelite is prayer.

When I asked to enter Carmel, they had to get permission from the archbishop because it was the law in Alabama that you couldn't have a mixed-race residence. I only learned about that later. My background is Creole. My grandmother's generation didn't have that much segregation because her father was French. He was an American citizen and he could vote. But by the time of our generation, we couldn't vote without taking a big test. There were all kinds of segregation, and that really did hurt. It hurt a lot.

Our Carmelites live a contemplative, cloistered life. That is, we have a papal enclosure, and we go out only for special occasions and with permission from the archbishop or the pope. And we always wear the habit. It was odd when most sisters took it off. I said, "Why take it off?" You know a policeman never takes off his uniform. And if a fireman takes off his uniform, he's in trouble. I even said that the first time the Carmelites got into modified habits. We have a modified habit now, and I don't think we'll ever take it off, because that habit makes us religious.

......................................................................................................

*Claretta Daniels graduated from Most Pure Heart of Mary High School in 1942. She taught kindergarten for 12 years there and third grade for three.*

......................................................................................................

It was just like a big family, Heart of Mary was. Everybody was so close to each other. I'd never even given it a thought about going to another school. I never questioned Mama. I still belong to Heart of Mary Parish. I've gone there all my life.

I was the first Miss Heart of Mary. I was so delighted because the football boys, they chose me. That's how they got their queen. It was a surprise to me. That was in high school. We won that game. I can't remember now who we played, it has been so long. That was the first year they had a Miss Heart of Mary. I was a senior. I played the trombone in the band all four years. At Xavier University I studied home economics.

*Claretta Daniels (seated left)*

One morning, when I was back in Mobile, I went to Mass and Father Vincent Warren asked me what I was going to do. So I said, "Well, I don't know." And he said, "Well, we're going to open up a kindergarten in January. Would you like to teach?" I said, "I sure would." So that's when I started teaching. 1944, I think it was. The kindergarten was next door to the rectory. The children were eager to learn and so sweet. I remember one year, I wonder how I did it. I had 52 children in my classroom. We had two tables, long tables. Half the children would sit at one table and the other half at the other table. I would go from table to table, helping them. And I'd read stories to them, in groups. They'd sit on the floor and I'd sit in one of their chairs. *The Three Little Bears* was my favorite, theirs too. Sometimes I'd let them play the story out after I would tell it to them. They were easy to handle. They really were.

I taught them how to print with straight lines and circles. And by the time they finished kindergarten, they knew how to print their name and address. I taught them about religion, about who made them. I'd tell them God made them. I'd teach them about the Blessed Mother and St. Joseph. I taught them their prayers: the Hail Mary, Now I Lay Me Down to Sleep, the night prayers. I enjoyed teaching kindergarten. I just feel like I touched them. And you know, they still, wherever I am, they'll come up to me and speak to me. "How you, Ms. Daniels?" I remember them, their little faces. I'll never forget any of them. There's something about young children, they just touch your heart.

When my first class graduated *[from 8th grade]*, I was there to see them graduate. Then they closed the kindergarten up. So I went and taught third for three years. That's when I became pregnant with my daughter. We were married ten years before we had children. I prayed so hard to get her. They call my girl the novena baby. I made so many novenas for her. That was Tonja. And I have a son, David Daniels the third. He's named after his daddy, who died six years ago. We were married 53 years. He was my first and only boyfriend. I had wanted to be a nun. Being around the sisters, from the first grade on, I just admired them. I wanted to be one. So when my boyfriend went into the service while I was at Xavier I said, "Well, if you don't come back, I'm going to be a nun." He came back in December, and we were married in June. I was always happy we married.

It didn't bother me to sit in the back of the cathedral. I didn't go that often to the white churches. The only thing that bothered me was the Feast of Christ the King. They had a parade for all the schools. I was so proud in grade school to be in the parade. But by the time I got to high school, it bothered me. We had to go at the end of the parade. The whites first, the blacks followed. They would be at the square before we entered, and then we would be so far away, you couldn't really enjoy the Mass. We were always on the sidewalks or in the streets.

We went through a lot of things. But I didn't get angry or bitter. I just didn't like it. That's the way it was when I was brought up. You just accept those things and say one day it's going to be better. And it is. I never got bitter at the church about anything. I just didn't like standing up in line and going at the end.

I remember in grade school, we always had a field day at Heart of Mary. All the grade schools came together, all the black Catholic schools. Bishop Toolen, he would come over, and he would throw pennies to the children. And they would get all down on the ground to get the pennies—down in the dirt! But I wouldn't get down. I didn't want to be scuffling for pennies. I never brought anything up to my students about race or anything. They were so young. Five years old. They didn't know the difference. And they never talked about it or asked me about it. Since they didn't ask, I didn't tell them. They just thought everybody was the same.

I remember one day, when I was taking my son to school, there were two men working in the street. One was standing over the other. The black man was down in the hole. So I told my son, "When you grow up, I want you to go to college, because I don't want anybody standing over you while you're doing your work." He said, "Mama, I could push him down!"

"No," I said. "I wouldn't want you to do that. That would be mean. But I want you to go to school where you won't have to do things like that, have anybody standing over you." And you know, he hasn't forgotten that. I didn't want them to be bitter. And they never have been. I never taught them to be bitter. Seemed like to me it was a sin.

# Most Pure Heart of Mary Catholic Church

Organized in 1899 as St. Anthony's Mission by Creoles of African descent. By 1901, Josephite priests Revs. Joseph St. Laurent and Louis Pastorelli had established a small school. The present church was completed in 1908 and dedicated as Most Pure Heart of Mary honoring the Blessed Mother. The parish and school were spiritual beacons during the civil rights movement hosting meetings for the Neighborhood Organized Workers-NOW. Diocesan priests and nuns participated in boycotts and marches in support of the black community. The parish continues as a spiritual home for Mobile's black Catholics.

The African-American Heritage Trail of Mobile

# III. Life with Jim Crow

*In the 1940s and and early 1950s few Mobilians, black or white were discussing civil rights. One who was talking was Father Albert Foley, a Jesuit sociology professor at Mobile's Spring Hill College. He was a prominent community activist who openly involved himself in inter-faith and ecumenical organizations and formed the Mobile Students Interracial Council. Foley constantly baited the local Ku Klux Klan and was much hated by the Klan in return. He also criticized Mobile Bishop Thomas Toolen for his unquestioning endorsement of the segregation system. In 1946 Toolen persuaded the Jesuits to get rid of this trouble-some priest; he was sent to North Carolina for graduate work, only to return in 1953, remaining at Spring Hill for the rest of his days. Better known to black Mobile citizens was John LeFlore, a layman who cam-paigned for voting rights in Mobile and in other cities in the gulf states as a representative of the NAACP. A third figure, Alex Herman, was a Heart of Mary parishioner and father of Alexis Herman, who worked largely behind the scenes to promote black voting opportunities.*

*None of these leaders had widespread visible support; whites for the most part resented them, and blacks did not want unnecessary trou-ble. As a result, the city remained relatively calm. Besides, Mobile's style of segregation was not a particularly harsh variety.*

.....................................................................................

*Life could proceed at a normal pace, explains* **Marion Lewis,** *a Heart of Mary 1965 graduate—as long as you obeyed the rules.*

.....................................................................................

In my family we were working class folks. We were not looking to change the world. We were just trying to make it day to day and not get harmed in the process. Our parents basically taught us a few things about survival. And a part of survival was don't put yourself in harm's way.

First, there are certain parts of town you didn't go to, plain and simple. And then if you're in a part of town, like downtown Mobile, where you couldn't help but interact with white people, there were certain things, certain unwritten rules that were made clear in my household.

If you're walking east and a group of white people is heading west, then you either need to cross the street or step out on the street and let them pass. You do not confront them, and that's it. If a white guy decides to hit you, you could not hit back. If you were caught, you could just protect yourself. Because if you struck him, it was over. You're in the wrong part of town, and they could do anything to you.

And you don't call white people by their first names. It was always Mr. This and Mrs. That.

And you have to know the whole idea about making eye contact. You make sure you don't. And do not come across as being belligerent, so you look down or look away.

And certainly you do not look at a white girl or white woman. You don't say anything to her.

Then there's the whole lunch counter thing. You go in the back door and get your stuff and go out the back door.

You absolutely obey any sign that says "Whites Only" or "Colored Only." Exceptions do not apply.

We didn't spend a lot of time talking about these things or thinking about white people in my family. It was understood there was certain behavior we were supposed to engage in. You accepted it and you stayed safe. Of course if something happened and the police were called in, you have to understand they're going to get you, and they're not going to do anything to the white people. If you got into a fight, you had the hell to pay, whether you were guilty or not. The police were going to take you to jail and beat the hell out of you. Everybody knew that's what would happen—if you made it to jail.

But really, we didn't live in fear. I didn't have a lot of negative interaction with white people. I didn't. It was because we stayed in our place. There were certain places you didn't go and certain things you didn't do.

As a family we didn't really encounter many problems. I personally didn't encounter many problems as far as segregation was concerned. Well, there was the bus thing and the colored and white water fountains, but we drank out of the one we wanted to, so it really didn't matter. I was from Down the Bay, and I took the bus to school for a time, but we didn't have many whites on the bus, because they were going in the opposite direction. I never heard any of my brothers or sisters saying anything about problems, nor did my parents complain. My daddy worked at Brookley Air Force base, and he never told me about any problems down there.

We just had to live with segregation. You know, we never had anybody on the city council or somebody black running for mayor. Actually, we didn't have enough money to run for anything. And you know, the blacks didn't have any supervisory jobs at that time. We were sort of like second-class citizens. Here's an example of that, I guess.

In high school we used to play football and stuff over in Crawford Park. On Sundays after Mass is when we used to go out there. It was a separate facility. We were on one side of the park on a little football field at the end. The white guys were on the other side. They had a place there where they could change clothes and all. But they always wanted to play us. So on Sundays we would play. We would play against them until somebody would call the police. And the police would come in and break us up.

We would play baseball and basketball out there too. And sometimes we would all mix up together, black and white, and play. Sometimes too we just played in the street with the white guys. We played football and baseball in the streets until the police came. Of course, we couldn't tell the police that we weren't doing anything wrong, just messing around. We couldn't do that. So when the police would start coming up the street, we would say, "Here come the white lilies!" At that time they had all white cars, and all the police were white. We didn't have any black policemen back then. So we'd just break up and go our own way. They didn't want to see us playing together.

........................................................................................

*Harold DuCloux, a 13-year graduate from Heart of Mary in 1965, hardly gave the very different lifestyles between black and white a thought until he experienced two "aha" moments.*

........................................................................................

Segregation was just a given in our lives. It was thoughtless; it wasn't something you had to learn. It was something that was always there. So it didn't really touch me because I didn't break any of the rules. But I clearly remember two conscious awakenings of segregation—two aha! moments.

I was 12 or 13 and riding the bus from downtown Mobile to my part of town. And I took a seat. I wasn't in the front but I wasn't all the way in the back either. And this teenager—he must have been about 17, got on the bus and said to me, "Go get in the back!" Now he had lots of seats to pick from, but he wanted to make me move, to go to the back of the bus, which I did. And it was one of the two times in my life that segregation touched me in a personal way. I was angry and hurt and scared all at the same time. But most of the time it wasn't that way. Nobody actually confronted you because you didn't break the rules and they didn't break the rules.

The other moment was when I was about ten. I was riding my bicycle to my grandmother's house. I lived in one black community; she lived in another black community, and there were several white communities in between. And as I'm riding this little kid comes along. He was on a tricycle; that's how young he was. And he said, "Nigger, get out of my way!" I was stunned. There wasn't a parent, there wasn't any adult around. I was going to go around him anyway, and then he just said that thing. That was my other "aha!" moment. Here I was. I thought I was obeying the rules, and all of a sudden I was different.

You know? I really was different. And I realized certain things applied to me or didn't apply to me that made me different.

· · · · · · · · · · · · · · · · · · · · · · · · · · · · · · · · · · · · · · · · · · · · · · · · · · · · · · · · · · · · · · · · · · · · · · · · · ·

*Patricia Kelly Lofton, who attended Heart of Mary for ten years, noticed the double standards of Southern life, but since they were never discussed, she took them for granted, only later realizing what they said about the races and about her until she was older.*

· · · · · · · · · · · · · · · · · · · · · · · · · · · · · · · · · · · · · · · · · · · · · · · · · · · · · · · · · · · · · · · · · · · · · · · · · ·

I grew up in an area called Carver Court. It was the first black residential community as far as parents buying homes in Mobile. And there was a Dairy Castle over there. They had a black water fountain and a white fountain. And to me, growing up, that was the norm. That's the way it was. And coming from Carver Court to Heart of Mary, I rode the bus. Coming one way it was fine but going back you had to sit in the back of the bus. We noticed the difference but didn't talk about it or even think about it. You know, growing up in your neighborhood, everything's fine. But as you grow up and start to move beyond that neighborhood, you pay more attention to the differences. For example, when you'd go to purchase something at the Dairy Castle, you never did sit on the inside of that Dairy Castle. We had to go up to the window. And the people were nice, and we purchased our little ham salad sandwiches and French fries and ice cream. But we always ate outside. That was the norm. It wasn't until later that we realized there's something wrong with that norm.

· · · · · · · · · · · · · · · · · · · · · · · · · · · · · · · · · · · · · · · · · · · · · · · · · · · · · · · · · · · · · · · · · · · · · · · · · ·

*Having to use separate water fountains and separate washrooms in public buildings left indelible memories with **Patricia Lewis Hardwick**. She remembers small details to this day.*

· · · · · · · · · · · · · · · · · · · · · · · · · · · · · · · · · · · · · · · · · · · · · · · · · · · · · · · · · · · · · · · · · · · · · · · · · ·

The biggest thing with me was catching the bus and having automatically to sit in the back with my sister, Chinester, four years younger than I. And if the back was full, then you had to stand up.

We were just young kids, and we had to stand sometimes and give white men our seats. And many times, if there were no more places in the back, they would make us stand up or get off and wait for the next bus.

Another thing that stands out in my mind from that period of time was that little white building over on the side of the civic square—Bienville Square they called it. There were two water fountains and one said white and one said colored. The white kids coming from Murphy and some of the other kids getting off the bus, they would go and deliberately break the black water fountains, which meant we had no access to water while we were waiting sometimes two hours or more down there in the heat. When I was about 15, one of my classmates, James Leatherwood, looked all around to make sure no one was watching and he drank from the white water fountain because they had broken the black one. Well, a policeman came up and beat that child down with a billy club for simply drinking from the white fountain.

And I remember the department store. My mother and father both had very exclusive tastes when it came to our clothes and shoes. My mother made practically all our clothes, but she would buy fabric and cloth from Hamill's Department Store, where we had an account. But at Hamill's the whites went in one door, they got on an elevator and they could go up, down or wherever. And there was one bathroom for white men and one for white women in the store. Blacks, if you had to go to the bathroom, you got on this other little elevator over in the corner, and the elevator stopped halfway between two floors, and there was a little, dark cubbyhole with one toilet in it. It was used by blacks, both men and women. You had to go in there and it had no place to wash your hands. You just had the toilet to use. I don't remember if there was even a light in there.

*The daily indignities could be borne fairly easily. Then there were those of a harsher variety.* **Leonard Stiell**, *HOM '68, recalls a brush with the law several years after graduation.*

This friend of mine from Abeline, Texas, asked me to ride with him to pick up his family. He had a wife and three young daughters. So I rode with him, and on the way back, his sister-in-law and her three children wanted to come with us and visit her own sister in Louisiana. So all ten of us loaded up in this old Pontiac GTO. And I was driving. We were getting ready to cross the Texas line into Louisiana, and a state trooper stopped me for speeding. I gave him my license. He looked at it. He looked at the tag on the car. He say, "Boy, get out of the car!" So I stepped out. He say, "Now come back here with me. You got an Alabama license. You got Louisiana tag on your car. And you in Texas. Boy, you fixin' to go to jail!" *[He laughs.]*

I didn't actually go to jail. I went to the jail house. They called the judge and the trooper told him what happened. We had to pay a fine. But I think it's a funny story. You know you see that kind of stuff on TV, but it actually happened to me. Just like that: "Boy get out of the car. Boy, you fixin' to go to jail." *[He laughs.]* I was 22 years old at the time. Once we paid the fine and left, it was funny. It was kind of scary when it was going on.

**Paulette Norvel Lewis** *recalls how Jim Crow took the joy out of a memorable family event.*

When I was growing up, the schools weren't integrated, and neither was the Catholic Church. My older brother wanted to be a priest, but when he applied to the Biloxi diocesan seminary they told him there was no place for him. Then a priest at our parish, who was a Josephite, asked him if he would go to the Josephites instead. He said yes. He went to their seminary, was ordained, and he eventually became the superior general of the Josephite order.

Wait, there's more. On the day in 1965 when my brother was going to be ordained in New Orleans, our parish rented a bus for the occasion. And we were on our way, black and white, on the bus and quite excited. And we were stopped on the highway by the police who thought we were freedom riders. They made us get off the bus and began to interrogate us and harass us. It wasn't until our parish priest, who was Caucasian, drove up, got out and talked to the police that they finally let us go. Oh, it was terrifying. It was very upsetting to my mother in particular. We did not want to be late. And we ended up being late anyhow. It was heartbreaking.

*Paulette Norvel*

................................................................................

*Just before her interview ended, **Dora Finley** was joined by Sister Patricia (Alberta) Caraher OP, one of her former teachers at the school. Dora wanted to talk about an incident that occurred early in her life, something she had spoken about only in recent years.*

................................................................................

Our neighborhood was like a little subdivision where the black people lived. When I was around eight years old I was going to the grocery store. And as I was walking I saw this pecan tree, and some pecans had dropped down on the sidewalk, so I picked up a couple and continued walking. Suddenly, this man came running out of a house carrying a shotgun. I ran, and he jumped in a truck and came after me. I ran to the corner. For a long time I blotted this out of my mind, but I can remember exactly where it was I ran to—it was the corner of Summerville Street and Wagner Street. I ran into this garage there because I was trying to hide. Well, he got out of his truck, he came into the garage with his shotgun and he put it up to my head. And he said, "You nigger, you better not ever steal my pecans again! I pay taxes on that tree." I remember it exactly. I can still see it. But I kept it a secret.

I didn't tell my daddy, because even though I was eight years old, I knew what was going to happen if I had told my daddy. I knew it would make trouble. He wouldn't have accepted what that man did. I realized that my daddy was going to go after those people and that they would kill him. I had sense enough to know that, and I kept it a secret. I just told mama about it like three or four years ago. She was flabbergasted. She said, "You never...!" I said, "Mama, I ain't never told nobody because I knew what would happen." But that's the society we lived in. For a long time I didn't go outside after that man did that to me. Nobody knew why I wouldn't go outside. There was another time I was walking, and these people were playing with a little baby about two or three years old. And they said, "Look, there go a nigger; go spit on her!" So there were some real hateful people. It wasn't just a little bit. It was some serious ignorance and hate that was going on.

But when I came to Heart of Mary, and all through school at Heart of Mary *[her voice gets very high and emotional here]*, if it had not been for y'all—this is what I'm trying to explain to you—I wouldn't have gotten this far. I was close to believing that all white people were bad, hateful. But I couldn't ever make that link, because y'all were in our lives.

*Alexis Herman, a 1965 Heart of Mary High School graduate, was probably more familiar with verbal abuse from white people than most Heart of Mary students. Her father, Alex Herman, was a significant political activist. He was also a veteran of the Negro Baseball League and knew the manager of the city's white team, the Mobile Bears, which played at Hartwell Field. He would occasionally take Alexis to a game.*

You see, my dad was the first African-American elected to any office in the deep South after Reconstruction, and his ward, Ward 10, was the one place black people could go and vote and not fear reprisal. I grew up under his wing and was very much aware as a child of what he had to fight and what he had to go through. At the baseball games, people would sometimes throw things at us, call us niggers or yell, "Get out, go home, you don't belong here!" And my dad would tell me, "Don't look back, just keep walking. Just look straight ahead.... It's their problem. It's not your problem. We have a right to be here just like they do." And when we would go home, he'd say, "Baby, you did good today, you did good. We'd go to Dairy Castle and he would reward me."

*But Alexis Herman's first introduction to abuse came much earlier in life and amid terrifying circumstances.*

Up until the Civil Rights movement, really in the 1960s, there was no grand community up-swell or protest. All the fight and energy in the community went into voter registration and getting the right to vote. The meetings about this were held over the bay in Daphne, one of those little bedroom communities far from the city. That's where Father Vincent Warren's parish was. Well, this particular night my dad had to go to one of these hush-hush meetings, and he took me along. I must have been about five or six and it was around Christmas because all the decorations and lights were up. My daddy always drove a DeSoto. That was his car, and he kept a silver pistol with a white pearl handle in the glove compartment. When there was going to be trouble in the community, he would have the gun sitting in the seat and he'd tell me to sit closer to the window.

We drive to Father Warren's. He goes to his meeting and I'm playing like I usually play. When the meeting is over, we get back in the car and we're driving back on these dirt roads, these back roads. During those days, this was a redneck community. I mean big redneck community. The Klan was there and the White Citizens' Council.

*Alexis Herman*

All of a sudden the road is blocked ahead of us, and lights come on all around from out of nowhere. My dad is forced to pull off to the side of the road. He takes out the gun and he says to me, "Alexis, I'm getting out of the car. You get under the dashboard on the floor. He took the gun and put it in my hand and he says, "If anybody opens the door, Papi wants you to pull the trigger." That's what I called him, Papi. I got on the floor under the dashboard like he told me. He gets out of the car and he locks me in there, and he walks away.

I don't know how long it was. I mean it still feels today like it was forever, but I could hear the voices, I could hear the noises—the car tires screeching and the yelling. I could hear all these horrible sounds. What I did not know was that the Klan had taken my dad and they were beating him up. Eventually, I heard Father Warren's voice calling, "Alexis, Alexis, it's okay. It's okay. It's Father Warren. I'm coming toward the car. I'm at the car. I'm at the car." And he opened the car door and lifted me out. He took the gun from me and cradled me in his arms. I looked over and saw them carrying my father away, a group of men. My dad had long straight black hair, and his hair was like falling in his face. And I could see his blood. I thought he was dead. Father Warren took me home.

I found out later, listening to stories, that the Klan knew there was a meeting that night at Father Warren's, and so when the meeting broke up they had set a trap for some of the men. Of course my dad was viewed as the ringleader. They knew which way he would come and they attacked him. Father Warren and a group of men decided to follow my dad back because everybody was worried there might be an ambush. They were able to break up the Klan beating and get my dad to the hospital. As it turned out, he wasn't seriously hurt. This was the very time civil rights actions were beginning. But in Mobile it was a very rare thing. We didn't have that kind of attention. But it was coming.

# IV. Pulling Together: Family and Community

*If there's anything that can enable a person to thrive in less-than-ideal circumstances, it's family, a caring, supportive family. In so many of the interviews for this book, including some that didn't make the final cut, Heart of Mary people talk of family and how it affected them. As one said, "Sometimes it felt like I was in this cold, choppy ocean and I was terrified. But I had a lifesaver to hang on to, and it was made up of all these people all hanging on in a big circle, all rocking in the waves. And it's my mother and father and my sisters and my grandfather and those old uncles and aunts. They're all there, and we're all shouting to one another, "Just hang on. We're gonna be okay."*

..........................................................................................

*These are stories from Heart of Mary families.*

..........................................................................................

***Patricia Lewis Hardwick***: All of us belonged to St. James Catholic Church, and all of us began school at St. James. On Aug. 10, 1959, we had a fire explosion in our house. My mother and my sister Gloria Stephana both had third degree burns. My father was second degree burned, and my mother was totally disabled for two and a half years. My youngest sister Chinester was getting ready to begin school in first grade. My oldest brother Roosevelt was going into his senior year at McGill. Well, no one was working in the home for a period of time after that. The decision was made that they couldn't keep us all in Catholic school, so my parents wanted Roosevelt to graduate with a Catholic foundation, and they wanted Chinester to begin with a Catholic foundation. Both were enrolled at Heart of Mary.

I particularly remember Sister Ronald (Thibodeau) from Heart of Mary coming by almost every day. My mother was a very religious person, and while she was in the hospital, her left leg, burnt literally to the bone, was drawn up and they could not bend it. They would put her in a soak every day, and mother tells me that Sister Ronald or one of the other nuns from Heart of Mary would be sitting outside her room while she was taking the soak. And she tells us that one day mother was saying the rosary, as she did several times a day, and it was like God just took the leg and straightened it out all by itself. When mother took a deep breath because the sudden change frightened her, the nun ran in and saw what was going on.

My sister lived for two weeks and died as a result of her burns. She was two years older than I. When the accident happened, Roosevelt was 15. Gloria was 12, I was ten, Norman was eight, Chinester was six, and we had a 20-month-old and a three-month-old.

The day my sister died, Sister Ronald had just left my mother and was checking on my sister in the hospital. And Father Beacock, who was our priest at St. James, was with her too. And he came to the house immediately after her passing with my father to tell us. But before telling us, we all said the rosary together, and then he and my father explained what had actually happened. And it was kind of difficult at first, you know, being a child, and having all of this to deal with. But as I grew and the family grew, it actually brought us closer together and gave us a great deal of strength.

And with all the children, Norman and I went into public school. I think I was about fourth grade and Norman was a year behind me. So Roosevelt was able to graduate and Chinester got her start on a good Catholic foundation. During the time my mother was recuperating, she stayed in the hospital about a year. I became mother to a three-month old, a 20-month old, a six-year old, an eight-year old and Roosevelt. I had to do the washing, cooking and ironing. Fortunately, we had been trained to do these things already.

Once mother came home she was still disabled; the hospital would send someone every day to change her bandages and things. So Norman and I, both being in public school right up the street from our house, would take turns coming home early. I would go to school and get out at 12 o'clock one day, and Norman would go to school and get out at 12 o'clock the next day. This way, my father who was working international Paper Co. could go to work. And actually, it all worked rather well; we all grew up healthy and wholesome.

Still, Sister Ronald and one of the other nuns would come almost every other day, and they would sit and pray with mother and entertain her and sometimes just sit in order to give us a chance to go to the park which was just across the street and give us a chance to play for a little while and literally be kids. Instead of our folks having to continue paying tuition for Roosevelt, he was such an outstanding student that Heart of Mary created a scholarship for him. St. James did the same thing for Chinester so she could continue that Catholic foundation. I think people looked at us sometimes and said, "Didn't you all get angry and bitter?" No, we didn't. We lived in that house for over 30 years after the fire, and we lost just my sister—the curtains, one mattress, but basically just her.

*Sr. Ronald Thibodeau OP*

Many years later, when my mother was 46 years old, after having two skin grafts on both legs, skin grafts on the upper thigh, skin grafts from around her stomach, she told Father Beacock she had seven children and didn't need any more. But she gave birth again to a beautiful son and named him Robert after Father Robert Beacock.

I graduated from Central high School in 1966 and went to Tuskegee University. Sister Ronald used to tell the students all the time, "Dream!" But my parents had already taught us that from birth: "Dream as big as you want," mother used to tell us. "You can be anything you want to be, whatever you want to be. But whatever, be the best." And my brother next to me used to say, "I don't know what I want to be." Mother said, "I don't care if you want to be a ditch digger. You just make sure you dig the best ditch." But Roosevelt graduated with his master's from Tuskegee in '64 and went on into the Air Force, became a commissioned officer and completed three tours at the Pentagon. He was the youngest black colonel ever in the Air Force at the time.

And in the late 1960s when Chinester was at Heart of Mary, I called home from Tuskegee to talk to China one day, and mother says, "Pat, you can't speak to her now. She's in jail again." I said, "In jail, mother! What in the world?" And the ironic thing was that the priests and nuns were marching with her and going to jail with her. She had become a leader in the Mobile civil rights activities.

Well, I was fortunate because of Roosevelt ahead of me and the other children coming behind. So I had to set the pace for them. I studied extra hard. Roosevelt had a full scholarship at Tuskegee, and Chinester full scholarship at Xavier in New Orleans. And her sophomore year she transferred to the University of Chicago. Of the seven living children, five of us have master's degrees or better. I have three master's. You know, I think we all did well because of that small, individual, caring atmosphere that we came out of.

..................................................................................................

*Dora Finley:* My mother taught American and World history at Central High School, and she started taking graduate degree courses in African-American studies during the summers at Wayne State University in Detroit. She stayed with her brother who lived there. And one day she came home with an Afro! She was the first woman he ever saw with an Afro.

When she taught, my mother believed in not just having the children spit out dates. She wanted them to have the historical context of the time. She wanted them to understand everything about the cultural aspects of what was going on in society—not just the good news. She'd even give them some of the dirt. She'd make it lively.

So she started to teach black history at Central, though it wasn't in the curriculum. There was no textbook because black history was completely outlawed and not recognized by the school board. So she made up these little pamphlet manuals, and she told the students to put them inside their textbooks. So while she was teaching, they could refer to their black history manuals. And she said, "If anyone comes in the classroom while we're teaching and discussing this material, just close your textbooks." She didn't want them to see the manuals and realize what she was actually teaching.

And from my father I got this strong, strong legacy of giving back to the community. As early as I can remember, when I was about five or six, we would go on Christmas to my mother's original home, Dr. Franklin's house, and had a big old Christmas dinner with Big Daddy. My mother had nine brothers and sisters, so it was a big family, and everybody had children. And then after we left, we went to father's family home. He grew up in Hickory Bottom and had lived two blocks from the Hickory Street dump.

My father would take me and my brother to the dump. I remember the first time he did it. He said, "I want y'all to see how, but for the grace of God, you could be living here. This is where you could be." And when the garbage trucks came, all the people living near the dump took off running toward the trucks because when they dumped the garbage, they wanted to be the first to go through it—with rats in the dump just running around. The people had made houses out of like cardboard. It looked like a shanty town, like what you might see in Africa. My father wanted us to have a sense that you have a duty to help people like this. Just "but for the grace of God," it could be you. "It's nothing that they've done wrong," he would say. "It was the circumstances they were born into." From an early age he instilled that sort of thinking in us. As I developed at Heart of Mary, the nuns built on this foundation. And it's this that directs my path and directs my life today. The culmination of these experiences is the feeling that I should do something with my life to make this a better place, to make a difference.

........................................................................................................

*Marion Lewis:* I played trumpet just about my whole life. In my family, just after the baby was born and they'd named the baby, they would ask, "What instrument are you going to play?" It was a given: you're going to play something if you're gonna live here. That's the tradition in my whole family, my extended family too. On both sides of my family, my mother, my father, especially on my father's side. The Lewis's were all musicians. That's what they did. Professional and jazz and gospel and church music. My father was in the choir at Heart of Mary. My grandfather was in the choir at the same time at Heart of

Mary, and they sang the six o'clock Mass every Sunday morning. My dad dragged me down there a couple Sundays a month to sing in the senior choir. We were on a sort of rotating basis. Either my older brother, myself or my two younger brothers would go, and we'd sit up in the choir and sing Latin. That was cool.

People talk all the time about family values and all that stuff. I haven't thought a lot about this, but I think the connectedness of family shapes you. Really, without thinking about it, you do certain things. You take care of family, and personally that has shaped me. Ever since I started at Heart of Mary, I wanted to become a teacher. I wanted to become a band director, a music teacher, etc. Now, as life has kind of played out, that's a lesser of what I do. What I have been involved in ever since is teaching in a broader sense—mentoring. I have several young folks that I've mentored a lot. I have volunteered to do a lot of working with teens and teaching teens life skills. Some of that is formal, some informal. What I do now professionally is coaching people career-wise. I am an executive coach, and I also coach people who have difficulties on the job, not behavior problems but more skills—anything from time management to delegation to how to communicate effectively. I got a lot of that from Heart of Mary. One of the things I remember was someone saying to me that she "studied people." That kind of started me thinking and I've studied people ever since then. I've done it formally, I've taken tons of courses. I've got a number of certifications. Reading people and understanding how they work, that's what I use a lot when I'm dealing with people. But the roots of that were in living in my family.

....................................................................................................

*Aurelia "Bootsie" Taylor Chestang:* My family was really involved with Heart of Mary. My father graduated from the elementary school. And then I have a sister, Addie Taylor, graduated in '46. Maxine Taylor graduated in '47. Autherine Taylor graduated in '48. Nona Taylor graduated in '53. Aurelia Taylor, that's me, graduated in '57. And Dorothea Taylor graduated in '58. Our parents were involved, oh yeah. They were in the fundraising and the cook-outs, the bazaars, the lawn parties, the Mardi Gras too. That's where they cook out on the avenue.

*Aurelia Taylor Chestang*

Because my daddy owned a grocery store, he would take us to school on his way to the store. And the part I liked about it is that our dad brought up our lunch to school every day. That's when Smith Bakery was in its hey day. They delivered fresh bread every day, every day. And the bread was sooo fresh! And it would be baloney or spiced ham with mustard. But the best part about that was the bread was really fresh.

And we all played an instrument in the band at school and at home. Addie and I played the trombone. Maxine played the clarinet. Autherine played the saxaphone. Herbert had a trumpet, I think. You could choose whatever instrument you wanted. But I chose the trombone because you're on the front line with the band. I said, shoot, I want the trombone because I wanted the front line.

Back in those days everything went on in your home, all the parties and special occasions went on in your home. And there were the times in the late 1940s and early 1950s when the Knights of Peter Claver would come to town for their big convention. We used to have to clean the whole house and shine the silver and get the china out. Mother would rent out the front bedroom, the living room. And somebody slept on the cot and another slept on the couch. Our family all had to sleep upstairs. You see, there were no hotels for blacks back then.

·········································································································································

**Sheila Flanagan:** My grandparents were founding members of St. James Catholic Church. On my mother's side of the family, everyone had always been Catholic. My mother and her two sisters all went to Catholic schools. It's just what people did in that branch of the family And my father, though he wasn't Catholic, always went to church with us. He had joined the Episcopal Church, but most Sundays he went with us. He never had any objections to us expressing our faith as Catholics. There was never a conflict like that in my childhood. For high school I went to Heart of Mary where my mother and her sisters went, and my sister too. At that time, a few blacks were starting to go to Bishop Toolen, but when it was my time, my mother sent me right to Heart of Mary. It was just automatically understood I'd be going there. There was no sea of democracy in that family.

My father worked at the Mobile Post Office, so he worked with John LeFlore [a leading Mobile civil rights pioneer]. Dad became very active in the rights movement. He was a founding member of the Non-Partisan Voters League. So I'm willing to say that my exposure to civil rights was greater than the average kid had because my sisters and I lived with it. My parents also had several businesses that they operated—a service station and a men's clothing store; they were very active in the community.

Ours was a household where civil rights and things of that kind were discussed at the dinner table. So I understood at a very early age the importance of civic responsibility, voting and being active in the community. And I understood the meaning of segregation and its impact on the community. I actually remember seeing a cross being burned by the Klan in my neighbor's yard when I was about eight or nine years old. A white family had just moved out and a black family moved in. And peering out of the venetian blinds, I said to my dad, "You should call the police!" He said, "No, the police are the Klan." He went and called the FBI.

........................................................................................................

*Joyce Cassino:* Growing up, we had some traditions in my family that we tended to celebrate with my grandmother and her sister, my grand aunt, not with my parents. One of the most memorable was Holy Thursday, which I still embrace, and I still cry at the service. It used to be grand ceremony at Heart of Mary—with the priest walking around with the Eucharist and the altar servers. It was just the most beautiful thing. And after the service that was the night when you had vigil at all the Mobile Catholic churches. They would all leave their doors open. And with my grandmother and great aunt, we would go around to the churches, black and white, and just stay and pray for ten or fifteen minutes.

It was special, going there and seeing how the different churches were decorated. And Holy Thursday night you got to go right up to the front of the churches. The restriction of blacks to the last few pews was lifted that night after the service. We were alright, we were all equal on that particular night. We could go to the cathedral, the basilica, Bishop Toolen's church, and walk up front and see all the gold and the grandeur of the altar. It was really an awesome experience to get that close and not be in the back of the church. We would stay out all night, to midnight, visiting every church.

*Class of 1965*

# V. An Inside View:
# Marion Lewis, Class of 1965

.......................................................................................................

*Marion Lewis was one of nine children in a family that was hard pressed to send everyone to a Catholic school. His father worked as an orderly, and the Lewis home was near the dump where Mobile's garbage was regularly dropped off. In this interview, Marion describes what classes and activities were like at Heart of Mary and the powerful impact the school had on him. He graduated from the high school in 1965.*

.......................................................................................................

Heart of Mary provided a good nurturing environment. Everybody knew you and knew your family, and everybody went an extra mile to make sure you got what your needed. Claretta Daniels [a lay teacher] was my first experience with the school. She was very straightforward; she taught us well. I looked forward to going to school. My whole family before me, the generation before me, and most of the generation before that, going back to my grandfather had all attended Heart of Mary. I couldn't wait to do what these folks had done. So the school, the nuns were not scary.

But from my perspective they were a little bit mysterious because they—we called them penguins—had these habits, and their heads were always covered. Always you wondered if they really had hair underneath. They were all starched and ironed and clean and had their rosaries hanging from their waists. Some of them actually prayed the rosary during class. A lot of times while we were working, they'd be fingering the beads, and their lips moving. But I was comfortable with them. Each had her own personality, some more religious than others, some very strict and authoritarian. I was comfortable with the whole range because, I guess, I was so familiar with it before I ever got there.

It was just expected in my family that we were going to go to Heart of Mary. There was no consideration of going to a public school. And there was no way in the world my family could have gone to Heart of Mary without being subsidized. My father was the only breadwinner, and he was an orderly and later became a male nurse at a hospital. But we had nine kids in the family (four boys followed by five girls), and we got the family plan, I think you paid for the first child and the rest got in for a couple dollars a month. So somebody was picking up the slack, and that message never escaped any of us. In my father's family there were 12 children. At least eight of them went to Heart

*Marion Lewis*

of Mary, and there was no way, no way my grandmother and grandfather paid for that because he was actually a janitor at Our Lady of Mercy Convent. He rode a bicycle, cleaned and scrubbed the floors, trimmed the hedges and did all the yard work downtown. So all of this was because we wanted a good education. It was a given that we would get a better education at Heart of Mary than if we went to a public school.

We had some good teachers in the grammar school, but the one that stands out for me was my seventh grade teacher Maybelle Braziel. Oh Lord, she was the most strict disciplinarian I have ever seen. She was tough. At times she used to call us "hoodlums" and "Hottentots." But she was an educator. She was bound and determined that we were going to grow up and be people the community could be proud of. She talked about going out into the world and being prepared from the standpoint of how you carry yourself, how you dress, how you talk.

She had very high expectations. She would ask you a question, and if you scratched your head, she would say, "Wait a minute. Why are you scratching your head? You don't scratch your head when you are thinking. You don't need to scratch your head." She was basically getting rid of all those habits that were sort of stereotypical of black folks. And if your shirt had a ring around the collar or you sweated a lot, she'd get on you. "Get out, go down to the restroom and get yourself cleaned up," If you go back and look at some of those stereotypical things on the old Amos and Andy show: the grinning, the shuffling of your feet, putting your hands in your pocket when you're talking, and scratching and rubbing your head. All those kinds of things she really addressed with, "You just don't behave that way!"

......................................................................................

*This school had definite rules and the competition was intense.*

......................................................................................

If you went to Heart of Mary grammar school, it wasn't a given that you could go on to the high school as well. There were only about 40 slots for the freshman class, and there were five or six other Catholic feeder schools into the high school. So if you do the math on that, there were probably 200 kids trying to get into 40 slots.

Everyone had to take an entrance exam, and based on the results they had a group they called the A Class and a group called the B Class. The A Class were the higher achievers. The curriculum for our A Class was much more strenuous and demanding. Besides English and history, we took algebra, biology, Latin and French. The others took more basic classes. The top 20 got into the A Class. The next 20 got into the B Class. And everybody else had to go to a public high school. We were the only black Catholic high school in town. Of course, the students were aware of these distinctions, but that's the way things were. You didn't question them. That's one of the unsaid things about the whole era.

Another reality, maybe a suspicion, was that if you were light-skinned—and I'm not—if you were fair-skinned and had wavy hair, you had an advantage as far as getting in the school was concerned. And if you were dark-skinned, you had less of a chance to get in. That's the way it was and we didn't question that either. I think part of the takeaway from that was that if you were darker-skinned you had to work harder. It was just a given that if you really wanted to make it and beat out the competition, you had to demonstrate that you were as smart or smarter than your fair-skinned counterparts. That's the way society was.

Everybody had to wear a uniform. Boys wore blue, starched and ironed pants, and the shirt was sort of a warm-season, white T-shirt on top of an undershirt. But during the fall and winter you had to wear a white shirt, either long-sleeved or short-sleeved. And then you had to wear a blue necktie and you had to have black shoes. Girls had blue skirts and a white top, and they wore what we called sandal oxfords.

I was in the A Class, and there were a lot of days I wish I wasn't. *[He laughs.]* It was tough. After taking Latin, I couldn't see straight. I just wanted to drive off a cliff. We had two years of Latin and then two years of French. I was so glad to get away from Latin, and all of a sudden I walk into a French class, and the nun is up there from day one speaking in French. And I'm like, "Okay, give me a break." I'm supposed to figure all this out, and I don't need this. But, you know, you fast forward and you get into college and you realize what was going on. I get all this in high school and algebra II and geometry and biology II and all that. I mean those were all college prep classes. We didn't know it at the time, but they were advanced courses. I got to college and my first two years, I didn't have to hit a lick. That was a plus, because I was able to focus on music, my real love.

I am a musician. That's what I wanted to do with my whole life, that and playing sports. And all the other stuff was getting in the way. So I did what I had to do to get by. I could have been much better but I wasn't that interested. And then the nuns got me caught up in these other things. I remember Sister Antoinetta (Marilyn Aiello) at the time. She was very interactive. You know, she brought animals into the classroom. We dissected frogs and all that kind of stuff. She had snakes in the aquarium. They were alive. And she just made the whole subject come alive. She was passionate about biology and you got caught up in her enthusiasm.

*There were high expectations from sisters and priests.*

The nuns we dealt with, they were young, they were energetic and they believed in us. They expected a lot from us and they helped us do whatever we had to do to be successful. I can't emphasize that enough. It was just like a family. They knew you by name. You couldn't get away with very much at all. *[He laughs.]* Clearly, they were preparing us for the future. I mean when you left Heart of Mary you were supposed to do something; you weren't being educated like that to do nothing. You were supposed to take some leadership role, no matter where you went. And I see it all the time when I see Heart of Mary alumni around the country in all kinds of situations. If there's a Heart of Mary person there they're very active, many times in leadership positions. It was just engrained in us that you were supposed to do something with your education.

It wasn't just the nuns either. Father John Harfmann (SSJ), who taught religion at the school and was an associate pastor at the church, got me and several other juniors and seniors to get involved in some of the bigger civic issues like poverty and homelessness. City officials at the time were talking about closing down the city dump, an area of about 15 to 20 acres, and putting up a compost facility there. But that would mean displacing more than 100 people who lived on the dump and depended on it.

I lived one block from the dump, so I knew what it was like. There were people who literally ate, slept, drank on the city dump. All these garbage trucks and construction trucks, small and big trailers, would come on the dump and had to be emptied. So these folks would jump on the trucks when they came into the dump and get off at the location. Then they'd unload all the stuff from the trucks, and the drivers would pay them a dollar or two for their work. And that's how they made their living. And there were food trucks from bakeries and from meat packing plants and from grocery stores. The folks would get whatever they dumped there and that's what they would eat. I mean all the garbage from the whole city would come there, and a lot of times these guys would go through household garbage and take whatever food or bones they could find. It was mostly men but some women too, even children who had been born on the dump. These people had built little wooden or cardboard one-room shacks where they lived.

Father Harfmann talked to us about what the city could and should do to find alternative living facilities for these people as well as getting them the psychological and vocational services they needed. I attended several public meetings with a commissioner and public works people present and reported to our student group what kind of progress they made. For me this was an exciting experience. I had never felt empowered to do anything like that before. And it was kind of dangerous to be involved in any kind of civic activities. You were supposed to be black and quiet and stay out of the way. Actually, I was in college by the time the dump problem was resolved, but the city did find some alternative places for the folks to live.

A little later a civil rights leader came to town, and Sister Claretus (Lorraine Rivers Tucker) asked me to attend a meeting about voter registration where he would be present. It was fascinating to be in the presence of these folks and hear the conversation about strategy. Frankly, the impression I got was how nervous I was and how calm they all were. You know it wasn't unheard of for the white suprema-cists to come by and shoot up a place if they knew about it. That experience was also exciting, and I reported on it to the class.

I think at Heart of Mary what we learned was how to discuss issues, how to debate—things I had never learned before. We had a debate team and part of the process was learning to think for yourself, becoming independent in thought. It was shaped by the spiritual values and virtues they taught us. I mean you couldn't help it. Every day you said prayers before every class, and you had religion every day—which was boring. Every day from grade school all the way through high school, it was like you had math and science and you had religion. I was more into music and sports.

When they had the debates, they would pull us all into the hall to watch. They were always debating topics of the day, but never seg-regation or race. The debate process was very structured and strict.

You had a certain amount of time to make your point, and you were coached on how to stand, how to dress, how to conduct yourself. Those were the kind of things that prepared us. It was for our good. And an important part of the process was that these nuns and Father Harfmann in particular were young and energetic. And they were pushing the limits, ours and theirs. I think they were a little bit rebellious too to a certain extent. So that's what we learned. It's one of the big things we walked away with from Heart of Mary.

................................................................................

*Students were taught to be assertive but don't push too hard.*

................................................................................

We had an issue with the requirement in our school that the majorettes for our band had to have these long skirts on. They couldn't wear pants, and the skirts came down below their knees. It was a religious thing, a Catholic thing. I was the junior class president and on the student council, so there were about seven of us who were leading the whole deal. We got together and circulated a petition. *[He laughs.]* We wanted the majorettes not to have these long skirts because we got ridiculed every time we were in a parade. It would always be the public schools. They had all these tight majorette uniforms on and pants and all that. And then we'd come marching down and we looked like a bunch of saints, and everybody jeered and laughed at us. Then we had to go home every day, and all the neighborhood kids would be laughing at us too.

Well, we got an edict from the principal, Sister Dismas (Slavin): "This is not going to happen. You need to stop the protest, you need to disband, and I'm not hearing any more about it." She came right into our religion class and said, "What are the two ugliest parts of the human body?" Well I didn't know; let me think. And she said, "The shoulder and the knee. Therefore, we decided we should keep these covered. So we need long sleeves and we need skirts that that cover the knees." And she walked out. We were disappointed. We thought we were going to make it happen, but we didn't.

We had some successes too. Also in my junior year we started what we called a talent show. We went around and organized folks and asked who wanted to be in the show. We had categories like singing, dancing, classical instrument playing, drama, the whole nine yards. And the thing took off. We asked for volunteers and the response was overwhelming. We literally had to audition people because we couldn't put all the acts on the stage. We advertised it and the response was huge. We publicized it in the public schools and we got a turnout we hadn't expected. The auditorium was overflowing. It started out as an idea and then we just put it together. The nuns had nothing to do with it. They let us do it. And you know, the last two years there we put it on as an evening affair.

*School was a cocoon preparing students for leadership.*

I am convinced that Heart of Mary formed me for a lot of the things I have done in my adult life—things that I don't believe I would have done without that education. One is my leadership. I'm an introvert, but Heart of Mary taught me—no matter if you were an introvert or extrovert—you push forward, you push yourself. You expect the best, and I don't mean that in material ways, but you are expected to step up and do something. I'm not the sort of person in the Catholic Church to sit back and say, "Let somebody else do it." And I see that all over with people I know who have gone to Heart of Mary. That's pretty universal.

I think the school was basically a cocoon. And when you get out there and find out the rest of the world doesn't care about you, you'd better get going on your own. Now that can be a problem if a school is too nurturing and you become too dependent on all that support. I didn't have that problem because since there wasn't a lot of individual nurturing going on with nine kids around—so you don't expect a lot individual attention in a large family. You have to fend for yourself; you understand if you want a new pair of socks or a new shirt or the latest whatever mom and dad aren't going to give it to you because they don't have it. So you need to get out there and find another way to earn some money on the side to get what your want or do without. So maybe because of that environment I come from I was okay with going out on my own.

Probably one of the highlights for me in high school was after Vatican II when the changes in the liturgy took place. And I have to go back to Father John Harfmann. He introduced English in the Mass instead of Latin, and then we could do more American music. So the guitars were starting up and the songs were fresh. It felt like our music. He got us involved with the liturgy. Up to that point, the Mass was boring as a nit. I mean boring. The priests couldn't preach and the homilies were terrible. And it wasn't feeding, it wasn't feeding anything. It was just something we had to do and was really not relevant.

Vatican II changed all that for me. I became much more engaged and much more active as a Catholic. I toyed with the idea of becoming a priest, only because of the role model Father Harfmann provided us. I listened to him as a mentor. We worked together on a number of projects. We did silk-screening of shirts for some program. Look, I'm a poor guy from Mobile, one block from the dump. I'd never heard of silk-screening before, and he showed us how to do it. Father Harfmann started a glee club and I joined it. And then he started a drama club and I got involved with drama. That's the first time ever I was on the stage. I was in *Green Pastures* and then we did another one called *You Can't Take It With You.* And he was the director of that. None of that was during school time; it was all after. So their involvement— the priest and the nuns—the fact that they cared and the way they just dove in there was so empowering.

A lot of this was going on during my senior year, and none of it had directly to do with segregation. But because of the times you just kind of dovetail with some of the things that were starting to happen with integration. That same year *[1964-1965]*, two of our students from Heart of Mary agreed to transfer to McGill institute. It was the beginning of desegregation.

*Joyce Cassino and Harold DuCloux*

# VI. Inside the School: Harold DuCloux, Class of 1966, and Joyce Cassino, Class of 1967

........................................................................................

*Both **Harold DuCloux and Joyce Cassino** spent 13 years at Heart of Mary School. They were married in 1968 and have been together since. In that spirit of unity, they were interviewed together about their years at Heart of Mary and immediately after.*

........................................................................................

**Harold:** Heart of Mary is like Hogwart's *[the school for wizards]* in the Harry Potter series. It's a special place where people attended school and were fortunate enough to get this really special educational experience that propelled us into a really special adult life.

**Joyce:** The special was the Heart of Mary community. My dad graduated from Most Pure Heart of Mary, so it wasn't unusual for us to have some of the same lay instructors. They were planted there, but the nuns moved in and out. Both my dad and I had Mrs. Braziel as our seventh grade teacher. I have five siblings, so I actually had at least two sisters precede me there. I had to contend with being compared with my sisters. Harold is an only child, so his experience was quite different.

**Harold:** Mrs. Braziel was a teacher we both shared, and she also taught my father and two of my aunts. But she taught in the public school system before she moved to the parochial system. So she taught my ancestors in the public system. I was always aware that this place was a special place—a kind of island where everything was different. We had white teachers who were nuns and a heavy emphasis on religion and spiritual growth. Off the island the standard conversation was peppered with profanity. It was the normal speech pattern. Think of it as almost another language. I was used to people using profanity around me all the time, but when people used it on the island, it was a shock. It was like, "We're at Heart of Mary. You can't use that word!" You could take two steps off the campus and use the word but not on the campus. Yeah, it was a different experience being on the campus and being off the campus.

*Joyce:* My take isn't quite the same. For me Heart of Mary was an oasis; I absolutely cherished it. We have different personalities. I am an introvert, so I didn't notice the differences outside so much as I cherished being on the island. And when I stepped off, I never compared it. In retrospect I knew the expectations were very high, but we were so immersed in it I guess we didn't realize the standards were so high for us. I was moving through those 13 years there with families I had known for a long time. And the nuns were more like friends to me. I know to some people they seemed as though they were on pedestals and untouchable, but I never saw the nuns or the priests as being untouchable or unapproachable. I was very comfortable around them because they had been in my life so long in the parish. They cared about us. I knew they were white. We talked about this, but I never saw their whiteness.

........................................................................................

*The unanswered question: What were the sisters really up to?*

........................................................................................

*Harold:* I'm just in awe at what the white nuns did. They weren't promoters of the social system of the South. They inherited it when they came here, so there was no great expectation about what they could achieve. They were basically on the island. They wore these long habits. (The transition to civilian clothes happened after my time.) I'm awed that they even came down here from the Midwest back then. It must have been like going to the moon for the nuns to go from Friday night fish fries and Kringles and the Green Bay Packers to the South where it was hot and everything was black and white—literally. I cannot imagine how much courage it took for young women to go,

"Yes, I'm going to follow my vow of obedience and go down South and do this thing."

*Joyce Cassino and Harold DuCloux, 1966*

And the thing they did was bring to us the Midwest expectation for education. They brought this Midwest model or paradigm. They didn't adapt it or change it; they preached it. And we responded to it. The Southern paradigm held that education for women was primarily to get a husband, and that really the educational system was designed for a few guys, right? In the South blacks don't really need a college education because they're not going to use it anyway. That was the paradigm, and the nuns came down here and said, "Everyone deserves a college education." When they counseled students in our era about going to college, they weren't thinking of southern colleges or historically black colleges like Florida A&M or Tuskegee. They were thinking of the University of Wisconsin and the University of Michigan and Northwestern and Notre Dame.

*Joyce:* I never knew until I reflected back that they had prepared me for a more global, diverse world, for the white, out-of-segregation world. I don't know if they were even conscious of that. They were directing us, and I felt like I just rose to the occasion. So when Sister Alberta raised that bar for me, I just moved up with it. Or when Sister Antonietta raised the bar, you would just rise with it. There was never any question of "I cannot do it." Those two were particularly instrumental in my life. They encouraged us to get involved in the programs and belong to clubs at the two white Catholic schools, Bishop Toolen and McGill. And I did, unquestionably and without hesitation. And I started to develop this competitive spirit with our white counterparts. And I gained so much insight and understanding that they were like us. They really broadened my scope, and I was very open to what they had to offer.

*Harold:* There was a spirit of competition within Heart of Mary itself. Once a year they would have this assembly, and they would hand out these medals to the best students in various subjects. And one year I wound up with six or seven medals, and I was like "Where's everybody else?" I didn't know until then that I had been responding to this competitive push. What they were communicating to us was, "You can do this. Here's a homework assignment in algebra or geometry or biology, and you can do this. I'm going to give you the basis to solve this equation." And so I solved the equation. I never thought about not being able to do something, not being able to solve an equation or finish a homework assignment. I never thought it was out of reach. But yeah, it was hard; it was very challenging.

*Joyce:* But so much of our instruction was simply amazing. For example, Sister Antonietta (Marilyn Aiello), who taught biology, took us out into a ditch. She's very short and she rolled up her sleeves and put on an apron and took us out of the building into this tar ditch that's part of a drainage area to collect specimens for class. Now the ditch is across the street from the school, not even a block away but still… she stepped off the island and she was still a nun. For us this was a real off-the-island experience. We were taking learning to another level. She was so excited and we were too, collecting stuff to take back, and we're going to do something with it under a microscope. And she's going, "Now we're gonna see what's underneath that over there"—an amazing teacher. It makes me happy just to think about it.

..............................................................................................

*The high pressure standards at HOM greatly influenced their college experience.*

..............................................................................................

*Harold:* When I went to Tuskegee I wanted to get into veterinary school. And the curriculum was designed so you could get into it after just two years in undergraduate school. But you had to take 20 college credit hours a semester to do it. Now nobody was doing that. They would break it up into four years, getting an undergrad degree in biology or math. Or if you tried to do it on the fast track, you had to go during the summer too because 20 hours of college credit is overwhelming. Well, I did it in two years and I didn't go to summer school. I did it because that's what I was supposed to do. I could do it because the course was designed for humans and I'm a human being. If the challenge is out there, I didn't even think about it. People would go, "You're taking 18 or 20 hours?" And I'd go, "Yeah, what?" *[He laughs.]* "I'm in college. That's what I'm supposed to do, right?"

*Joyce:* Until I went to college, I didn't realize how high the standard was at Heart of Mary. We did not have to study, literally, except for Spanish because we had taken Latin and French in high school. I was so impressed with how my life was impacted by the nuns. It was their spirituality, I guess—the quietness and peace they walked around with, except when people like Harold antagonized them. *[She laughs.]* I don't even know if there was stress in their lives or if they insulated themselves from the stress. I tried to pick up a lot of that as well.

I was more into fine arts, language arts, English in high school. I excelled in those particular areas, while Harold is a very scientific mathematician kind of person. So we had different areas of interest. And sitting down here talking about this, I realize we were so insulated from the segregation system we lived in. Insulated because we were excelling so much. I was more aware than Harold of what was going on with the Civil Rights Act and the changes that were going to be made. And we have wondered if the nuns were cognizant that they were preparing us for that, for the time when the veil would be lifted and we would be able to compete in integrated Mobile with our white counterparts. So that's a quandary: How did these young nuns come into segregated Mobile and, either consciously or unconsciously, start preparing us for the future? Because what they did was amazing. What happened is that they started to nurture what was inevitable for me. I'm a social worker, and so it seemed very natural for me to be nudged into social justice kinds of things. I picked up the nuns' encouragement and engaged in all of those kinds of activities. I was really aware of the civil rights movement.

*Civil segregation they could understand. Church segregation was something else.*

*Harold:* The church issue about having to sit in the last pews ticks me off even now. I feel that—not the Catholic Church in general, but certainly the diocese of Mobile—owes both its black parishioners and its white parishioners an apology for what they did during that time. I could understand the school system. That was logical to me, because there weren't intermixed schools. But I'm hurt by what happened behind the doors when you went to church. Every time I think about it I get hurt all over again.

*Joyce:* What hurts me the most was this talking out of both sides of your mouth at that time. We were all created equal under God, but we weren't. At least that's not the way we acted. It's one of those faith issues that to me is a black spot on the Catholic Church that will be there until I die. This judgment about the non-Catholic churches made no sense to me. When we would walk home down Davis Avenue we'd see a lot of churches, but we were not supposed to look at them. You had to walk straight ahead, and of course your curiosity, your eyes, would wander. But you feel you couldn't look over there because you're going to hell if you look at that church. And we were definitely not to go inside the churches. It was a conundrum for me, because I belonged to a brownie troop, and that's where we met, in the non-Catholic church. And I did. But we met in the basement of the church, so I figured I was not going to hell just for going into the basement of the church.

*Harold:* Yes, it was very conflictive. I can't be part of the white community. And I can't be part of these other black churches either. So where am I? It was a bitter time. Heart of Mary was a different experience, but Catholicism was extremely confusing and hurting. And here's where the conflict struck home. Three of my four grandparents were not Catholics. And so as a kid sometimes I would just start crying for them, and I'd almost be inconsolable because it was a secret. I was crying for them because I knew they were going to hell, and I couldn't tell them they were going to hell. There never was any discussion. If there had been, I suppose I could have said, "How is it that my grandparents are going to hell?" But the subject was never opened. I guess I had a six-year-old mind trying to navigate thousands of years of spiritual speculation. So I had to build some bridges across ravines that never existed.

*Joyce:* We went through a lot of priests at Heart of Mary. We may have gone through five or six priests when we were at the high school, and we never did develop a relationship. Some you could be comfortable with, some not. You could immediately tell if the priest was uncomfortable with children, and I'm still sensitive to that to this day. They were all white.

*Harold:* Later on the parish had a black priest for a while, but he didn't work out. It's sort of funny and ironic that the first black pastor of Heart of Mary didn't do well because he was black. He was too black. He had African vestments, had a black Jesus on the cross, and he was very immersed in the African-American experience and our African roots. And that was too foreign for our parents. They weren't comfortable with him; they were barely comfortable being Negroes and.... *[He laughs.]*

*Joyce:* The message we got wasn't controversial at all. It wasn't black or white. It was based purely on the gospel. Blackness didn't enter into our social system or our notion of justice until integration became an issue.

*Harold:* So I'd say most of our Catholic teaching was done by the example of the nuns, how they taught, how they lived. It was the nuns.

*Joyce:* That's a good point, a very good point.

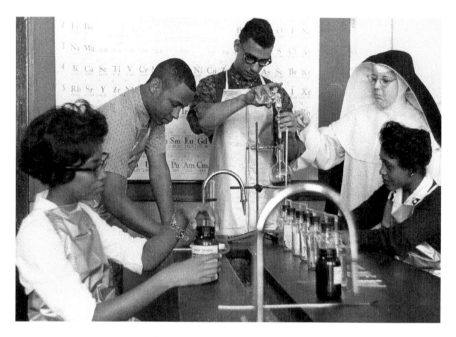

*Chemistry class in early 1960s*

# VII. An Inside View: Pamela Hutchinson, Class of 1968

*Pamela Donald Hutchinson spent 11 years at Heart of Mary,
finishing in the high school's last senior graduating class in 1968. She is
the daughter of Jacqueline Rice, who graduated from HOM in 1941. In
this interview Pam discusses her wide range of school experiences and
her unique take on classes and school activities.*

I look back at my friends, my friendships for 40-some years. I'm still
connected to so many, and that says a lot. I asked my daughter if she
was going to go back to St. Joe's *[her school in Baton Rouge]* for any
of the activities they have for grads and alums, and she said, "Mom,
I don't have that connect. Maybe if it had been like Heart of Mary I'd
feel differently." Well, that kind of warmed my heart because the only
thing she knows about Heart of Mary is the stories she's heard. She
knows what we had. We would always go back to Heart of Mary. It's
just part of who I am. It's part of my roots.

I went there because my mother was from a family generations
Catholic. You're a Catholic, right? You have kids, you send them to a
Catholic school. She was determined to do that. Heart of Mary was
also the choice because that was the side of town we were living on,
the north side.

I remember best my second grade and the teachers in those fly-
ing nun outfits. I remember Sister Valerian (Elizabeth Barribeau). She
was nice but then she was strict. I remember the first time I got in
trouble with her and how she used to poke you in the shoulder and it
was like that index finger felt like it was going through you. It straightened you up—you know what I'm saying? I can see myself in that
classroom, and I can see her walking around. I can see the windows.

And they're still there.

We were all sitting at desks. I'd say there were about 30 of us. I can see the blackboard and the cursive alphabet over the top of the blackboard, and the flag and all the little tools Sister Valerian used to teach with. And I can see her walking. She walked very slowly; she walked like back on her heels. We thought those nuns were old, but they were really young. You know, when you're seven, eight, nine, 27 is old. I remember Sister Valerian keeping order in her classroom because we were scared of her. When she did get upset, like I said, she would poke you and your shoulder would just kind of give. You've got to remember we were little people then. So I tried to be good in her class. *[She laughs.]*

...................................................................................................

*In the 1960s, Heart of Mary college-preparatory classes were the norm. Pam was one who reacted with energy and enthusiasm.*

...................................................................................................

In fifth grade Sister Alberta (Patricia Caraher), who we now call Patty, came along. She was a great teacher and we learned a lot from her. The next year we moved to sixth grade, and boom, they moved her to sixth grade. Then when we got to the high school, she was sent to teach in the high school, so I had her for English all four years of high school. I told her one time, "You made me suffer through *Pride and Prejudice, Huckleberry Finn* and *Jane Eyre*." She did. She made us read books and then we would have to do essay tests discussing the plots, the settings, whatever. She taught us how to write. I appreciate that woman because she taught me how to write. She taught so much in depth about writing—so much more than anybody gets from multiple-choice tests.

She was almost always in a good mood, always happy. But when she was upset, when she would come into our homeroom and we were cutting up, we'd know it. She would slam a book down on the desk. Pow! And it just commanded respect. But that was rare. She had so much patience with us. It's like she identified the talents and the gifts and the skills of each of us. And she tried to develop that and help grow that. And if she was working with one student, I don't think anyone felt jealousy. It's like she gave me what I needed and she gave Debra what she needed and Caroline what she needed. She was always encouraging me to go and do. If I had an idea, I'd go talk to her about it, and she was always my biggest supporter. Mom would call Sister Patty sometimes and say, "Can you tell me what's going on with my daughter?" *[She laughs.]*

The other nuns were great too. Whatever you told them, your secrets were good with the nuns. I'm going to share this story with you. I hope you won't think it's gross. But Sister Jane (D'Aza Bray) was my biology teacher, and this was at the time when tampons and Tampax had come onto the scene. And of course I wanted to be New Age. My mother said, "Absolutely not. Are you kidding? No, you will not use them. That's why they make these Kotex pads." Well, I decided to do it anyway, but I accidentally pulled the string loose. I didn't know who I was going to tell, and I was a nervous wreck. After what mom said, I couldn't go to her. So I said, "Sister Jane. I got a problem." I told her what happened and she said, "Well you know what that means." I said, "What?" She said, "You're going to have to go up there and get it." I said, "With what?" She said, "With your fingers." I was like, "Sister Jane, I can't do that." She said, "Oh, you're gonna have to do that." *[She laughs.]* So she helped me do that, you know what I'm saying? It was just that you felt comfortable to go to the nuns in that way. They were like your buds.

........................................................................................................

*In the midst of her education, Pam discovers a talent she did not know she had.*

........................................................................................................

In our junior year we were doing a dramatic interpretation of *Medea*, Greek mythology. They wanted me to play Medea, the lead role. Sister Bernardo (Cashman) told me what it was about. You know the woman was crazy; she killed her kids and blah, blah, and all this good stuff. So I was like, this is easy, I can do this. Well, I did *Medea*. I did it from a dramatic interpretation we read, and I remember Sister

Patty sent me to Spring Hill College to compete with others. They were having this one-act-play competiton for a lot of schools.

This was my first time, feeling like, "Oh, my God, I am a colored kid in a white environment." I remember being scared, feeling fear with the whole surroundings. In fact, we didn't have a car then, and to this day, I don't know how I even got out to Spring Hill College. But I did. I got out there and I did my dramatic interp, and I think I came in third. I've always thought I came in third because I wasn't comfortable with the environment, being 16 or 17. But I found the courage to stay there even though I was surrounded with white people. You know I wasn't used to that.

I'm not sure if it was Sister Bernardo or Sister Patty who wanted me to do it, but that doesn't matter. They were all in cahoots because they were all English literature teachers. Then later we had a competition with the four Catholic high schools, and once again it was this one-act play festival. So we did that play again, and I was like, "Okay, y'all, we're going over there to kick butt." This time I'm inspired. I want to go over there and show these people we can compete, we can measure up. Well anyway, we did, we went. Sister Bernardo received best director. I received best actress. We went in there and showed our stuff, and this was quite an experience for white people too, because they weren't used to being around us either. In segregation you just didn't interact. So I remember being so proud, and any time after that when we did field day competitions, any time we were up against Toolen or any of the other white schools, I wanted to do my best. I wanted to show them we can compete in this arena or any arena you put out there. Being that young, I guess that, without realizing it, this was my way of trying to eradicate racism in a positive way.

........................................................................................

*The one subject that gave Pam the most trouble was religion. The school encouraged logical thinking, asking questions and open discussion. Here she encounters attitudes that seem to stifle openness.*

........................................................................................

From the Back of the Pews to the Head of the Class

*Pamela Donald Hutchinson*

I kept telling them the *Book of Genesis* made no sense to me. You're telling me because some woman gave a man an apple and he bit into it, and now we're suffering forever. I said, "Can you all come up with a better story?" *[She laughs.]* Is the Bible really true? Is this how the world was created? Is this it or is there some other reason why we're the way we are?" I didn't know what I was hitting on. When I look back, I think some of my friends were upset with me. I told them, "Well, it's a very good book written by many men and, as authors of books do sometimes, they sensationalize. They put in things that aren't really true. So when you read it, you can't read it literally. You have to read it carefully and take from it whatever can impact your life."

You can't go around saying, "God said this and God said that...." No, he didn't. Paul said that God said—and I don't know for sure if God said that. You know what I'm saying? Another thing I had a problem with was confession. And I asked, the teachers, "Why do I have to go tell the priests my confession when I can go directly to God myself?" I guess back then they weren't used to people questioning religion or questioning the Catholic Church. There were certain things you had to believe, and questions that all had set answers for you. What is mortal sin? What is venial sin? Why can't you eat before you go to Mass? You had all these rules and regs and da, da, da. And I just thought some of them did not make sense. And one day Sister Antonietta (Marilyn Aiello) put me out of religion class. Actually, I got put out of a couple classes at Heart of Mary because I was questioning things. I always got back in, but I was always questioning. I guess back then I was looked at as a rebellious kid.

Actually, they wanted us to ask questions and discuss and debate at Heart of Mary about almost everything—almost. When it came to religion, it wasn't the same. You didn't question the Catholic faith. My folks didn't. My aunts and all didn't. Sometimes I think I was kind of ahead of myself by the time I went off to college. I was wearing purples and reds and black and white checked raincoats or whatever, and I could tell girls used to look at me and say, "She's kind of weird." And a lot of what I was wearing in the 1960s is back and popular now. I guess I felt a little on the outside because I was the only one doing it.

When I was in my sophomore year, maybe my junior year, I asked my mother about maybe switching schools because Heart of Mary was so conservative when it came to the social scene. We didn't have a decent football team. We didn't have a lot of dances and all that good stuff. Whereas down the street, Central High School had all of that: different club dances and great activities. And my mother said, "You're not going to Central under any circumstances. No, absolutely not!" And then she said, "You want to go to Central? You can go during the summer. Go to summer school there." So I did. And I can remember thinking after that summer how fortunate I was to be at Heart of Mary where I was getting one of the best educations around. The teachers at Central weren't about the business of making sure you were learning. We played a lot. The teacher might come in and say, "Okay, y'all be quiet," or "Write this paragraph." Anything to keep us busy and not bother them. We played around and we weren't really interested in learning. I realized from that I didn't want to go to Central. I did want to stay at Heart of Mary.

..................................................................................................

*Yet despite all her questions and uncertainties, there were some very visible, basic realities in her life that Pam never thought about—like the real meaning and implications of segregation. In fact, she admits, she didn't see them until she was almost out of high school.*

..................................................................................................

You know, I didn't have a real sense that these nuns were Caucasian or what racism and segregation were all about until my senior year in high school. When Martin Luther King was shot and killed, at that moment, all of a sudden I *got* racism! I'm like I got this, I got this. I went to school the next day. I walk into Sister Patty's classroom and I'm looking at her with this strange look. She looks at me and she says, "Well, what's wrong with you?" And I said, "You're white." And she just kind of popped me with a piece of paper, and she was like, "You just figured that out?" and she walked off. Yeah, I did. I really did just figure that out. *[She laughs.]* We had never encountered nuns who put us down or ever made us feel like we were inferior or that the kids over at Toolen and McGill were better than us. So we never thought of the sisters as Caucasians.

I always took segregation as a given. I grew up around black people and black families. Hilary Clinton said it: "It takes a village...." The village had been raising kids where I come from. So I grew up around black business owners who repaired shoes and TVs and sold us groceries. So the life I had was good. I didn't know or want more. For Christmas you listed two or three things and you got those things and you were excited. It was as if this was the good life.

When I was younger, I would go to the movie theatres or the train stations or the bus stations, and I would always sneak around. And when people weren't looking, I would go and peek in the restaurants and see what they looked like. At the theatres I would sneak down to the second floor to see their concession stand. Now mind you, they always had more, it was always plush. But I was like, so that's how it looks. I don't remember saying, "Oh wow! I want to go in there." Because as far as I was concerned, we had a good life here. It wasn't until King was killed that all of a sudden I realized what all of those "Colored only" signs meant and what those "White only" signs meant.

I have to go back to when I was about five or six, and the Montgomery bus boycott extended down into Mobile. Black business owners and other people too would gas up their cars and take people where they needed to go and keep them off the bus. Because we never had a lot of money, any opportunity to ride the bus was a big deal for me. I remember this particular day the bus was coming, and my mom said, "We can't ride it." When I asked why, she said, "We can't ride the bus, baby. We just can't do it." I remember being disappointed and asking why. And she never would tell me.

I think maybe she thought I was too young and wouldn't understand it. But it wasn't only that. My mom and people from that generation, they were just kind of scared to buck the system. So they just didn't talk about it. But then they followed through on the action; they were not going to ride the bus during the boycott. Once Martin Luther King was killed, I realized what was going on and how torn this country was. I mean it just came crashing down on me like you wouldn't believe.

I remember being 13 and watching Governor George Wallace standing in the door of the University of Alabama. It was on TV. I couldn't understand why he was doing that and why he wouldn't let that girl in. But you see I just wasn't there yet on the whole integration and segregation thing, you know? Even in my junior year at Heart of Mary, when they talked to me about going over to Bishop Toolen High School and being one of the trailblazers, I was like, "I'm not going over there." And when they asked me why I didn't want to go, I said, "Because I don't." And I remember also saying, "Because I won't have the opportunity to do all the things I'm doing at Heart of Mary. Besides. it's a tradition in our family. We graduate from Heart of Mary."

I think the unopposed reality of segregation in our lives kept us from seeing what King had been trying to achieve. I knew who he was and what he did, but it did not impact me that he was trying to restore and bring about human rights. I mean human rights first, then civil rights. It did not impact me that he was trying to heal the divide of racism in this country—until he died. As far as I was concerned, I was getting one of the best educations. I had the best teachers. We were involved, we were doing things, we could compete, we were at the top of our game. In a way we were just kind of shielded from the real world. Then he dies. The city is in uproar. They're burning buildings, they're burning stores. And for the first time in my life, I'm realizing, Oh my God, we have a serious problem here! I realize there are people who don't like me because of the way I look. I can't go to certain places and do certain things because in this system I have no right to do this or go there. Whereas before, I didn't feel that. My life was good. I didn't understand there was a lot right here that had to be done.

I'm so proud I was able to graduate from Heart of Mary, given the hard time my mother was having just to hold things together. I remember the tuition was $14 a month. You'd think it was $1,400 every month the way she had to scrape to get the money together. When we had her 90th birthday party last year, I was doing a little presentation of her life, how she went to Heart of Mary, grew up and raised me. And I told how hard it was for her to come up with the $23 for my class ring. I was dating Sam Jones then. He was my first boyfriend; now he's the mayor of Mobile. Anyhow, back then we used to exchange rings. So I had his big Central class ring around my neck, but I told him, "You can't have my ring. As hard as my mama worked for this ring, if I lose it she would have a fit. I cannot give you my ring." And as I finished the presentation, I said, "So, Mom, tonight I proudly wear my ring," and I held my hand up. And I still have the ring.

*Group of sophomores in 1960s*

*Sisters Salvator Falardeau, Columba Prendergast, Wilima Buckley,*
*Raymond Pennafort (Ursula) Walsh, Audrey Kerber,*
*Nada (Geraldine) Mye, Valerian (Elizabeth) Barribeau,*
*Melissa Waters, Marie Denise Dwyer,*
*Marianus McDonald, Alexine Stander,*
*Ronald Thibodeau, Cyrinus Randerson*

# VIII. The Staff:
# Raising Expectations

..................................................................................................................

*It's generally agreed the high school had an outstanding staff during most of its existence. Here some of the key people talk about what they were trying to do and what they achieved.* **Sister Alberta (Patricia or Patty) Caraher** *grew up in Chicago and had been teaching at a Catholic school in the Bronx in New York City before arriving at Heart of Mary.*

..................................................................................................................

On August 4, 1960, I got a message *[from the Dominican motherhouse in Sinsinawa, Wisconsin]* that I was being transferred to Mobile, Alabama. I said, "Oh, I gotta look this up on the map. I don't know where it is." So I find out it's Heart of Mary and it's an all-black school. I called my mother, and she said, "Oh, you chose it. I know you chose it. I know you want to be there. It's just like you to want to be there." I said I had no idea I would be going there. She was really upset. I suppose in her mind I was really going to the bottom of society. Why would you ever do that? You've got an education. Well, my family always went on a vacation trip in the fall. And just one month after I got to Alabama, I get a phone call from my mother. "We're down in Biloxi, Mississippi. And we're gonna come over to see you!" I said, "What?" They had to check it out. (I'm starting to cry.) And then they were fine once they saw that I was happy and I lived with such wonderful people and they got to know some of the children.

I came to Mobile when I was 25 in 1960 and left when I was 40 in 1975. So my time there spanned a very significant moment in the history of African-Americans in Mobile. It was also a very significant moment in our country in terms of civil rights. I got formed first of all by Dora Finley's mother, who really helped me a lot. My students formed me and their parents formed me. And the whole culture formed me. And the prevailing sense of injustice and the drive toward justice formed me. I had to learn what it meant to be black and to live in a white world and yet not to be accepted by that white world. I wanted to be with them in feeling the injustice of the whole thing. And I wanted to be with them in such a way that I could make a difference. And I thought I could make more of a difference because I was white. Our community that lived at Heart of Mary convent had a strong sense of we're gonna make a difference in this society, in this local community. We're going to stand up for this African-American community, and it's going to pit us against the white community. When you have one common mission and you've got 13 of us, and we're all together in one common mission, it is an extraordinary thing. It really is.

When I first got there we had these events that were sponsored by the archdiocese, and one was in an outdoor auditorium. So I walk in and I see the sign "Colored Schools." Colored schools? This is a Catholic event. And I was kind of appalled and hurt. And one of our sisters, Sister Wilma (Buckley), put her hand up and ripped it off the wall. I like to say the word "ripped" because that's exactly what she did. That image has stayed with me forever, because it was such an act of courage. And I thought wow—the nerve, the guts to do it. But that image and the realization that the church is complicit in this segregation touched me deeply. The church is complicit in injustice. The church itself is part of this culture. You know, we thought we were doing wonderfully well by having a black school and having a black church. We're giving them all this!

The word that comes to me is "paternalistic." I'm going to help these people? All of a sudden I felt I have experienced the whole systemic thing. I didn't quite get it until I saw how the whole system is favoring the white community, and the thing is so much bigger than I thought it was.

*Sister Patty learns she's black!*

*Sister Alberta (Patricia Caraher)*

Oh my gosh, my life would be so different if I hadn't come to Mobile. African-Americans have deep within themselves some kind of soul. I mean soul in a couple of different ways. It's something we westerners have lost in our busy-ness of life, and I feel in Mobile I touched a place in myself that probably was an ancient place that once my Irish ancestors knew. *[There is a long pause.]* It was some kind of a primitive understanding of God and spirit and life and goodness and community. Oh, community was so important to the people here, and they just kind of enveloped me. I was just embraced in my otherness with that deep river of compassion and river of mercy that I will always be grateful for. It set me on a path. I tend to be a head person. But in Mobile I was on an experiential path. It wasn't just in my head. I experienced it with these people.

I'm reminded of a story when I was teaching fifth grade. There were two cousins, and they were arguing in the playground. I said, "What is this about?" And one of them says, "Shirley says you're white." And Shirley says, "Rose says you're colored." Well, I was totally taken aback. And the more I thought about it, I realized, my gosh, I've made it. *I have made it.* They think I'm black. So that night—this is the funniest thing—I had a dream in which I looked in the mirror and, sure enough, I was black. I felt so accepted. It sounds strange, but as time went on, I realized that black doesn't necessarily mean just skin color. At a deeper level, it means you're one of us. They didn't have any other white people in their lives. So they're telling me, "You cannot be white. You cannot be white because white people are like x,y and z. You have to be colored."

What I wanted most was for them to make it in the white society. I taught English, and we did a lot of literature. But writing and speaking were important. So I made them do a lot of that too. I said, "You can speak your natural way at home and in your neighborhood. It's so beautiful; it's so colorful." And they could give speeches. Wow, they could! I wanted my students to make it. But to do that they had to give up something, surrender something, deny something. They had to learn to live in both worlds. That was part of my thing. "This wonderful language you use is not going to make it when you look for a job in the professional world. So you have to learn this other language. I'm not putting down your language. I want you to use it in your homes, your family, your community." Still, there was something inside me that felt always conflicted about that.

Spiritually, I probably learned more from them about who God is than they learned from me. Because I had a kind of narrow sense of who God is. I hadn't taken God out of the box yet. But in a way they had, because of their spirituality. As Catholics, God was in the box for them. But there was this other part of their spirituality that was much wider and deeper and broader than the box could hold, connecting to a spirit that was so compassionate, so loving. It's about putting my trust in God, about God walking with me.

I wanted them to talk so articulately about this so they could speak up against the injustices they were experiencing. I wanted them to be able to say, "My voice will be heard."

For them, Jesus is an extremely important God figure. This is how they see it: Jesus suffered; I'm suffering. There's a powerful link there. And it leads to downright total trust in God that it's all going to be okay. I'm going to be okay. I'm going to be okay in this world. It's a kind of abandonment to God.

So what they taught me, I guess, is trust—a deep faith. And that's great. But at the same time I wanted them to get out of that. A little too much trust. Too much abandonment. Too much "this is my lot in life"! No, it's *not* your lot in life, and this is *not* where God wants you to be! This is what society does to people who are subjugated: teach them to "be where God planted you," teach them that "God loves you to remain in the position you're in." No! that's *not* true. They had to get beyond that God to the God of justice and the God of resurrection who is going to burst forth in their own voice and in their own identity and their own community's strength and power. This is what I wanted. It takes a lifetime, I suppose.

My own link to Jesus goes way back to when I was very little. I lived in a second-floor apartment in Chicago with my mother, my aunt, my two uncles and my grandmother, who was from Ireland. This was during the Depression, and people used to come up to our tiny little porch for bread. "Can you help us out?" She always had me go on the porch with them, and she always told me, "You know, one of them is Jesus." Of course at my age I didn't know much about Jesus, but if grandmother says someone is Jesus, he must be someone special. So I'm sitting there with these men as they eat, realizing one of them is special. So they all became special in a sense. That was a grounding for me, a grounding I have never let go of. I brought it to Mobile and continue to bring it wherever I go.

................................................

***Sister Antonietta (Marilyn Aiello)*** *remembers the day in 1962 when, at the age of 24, she traveled to Mobile, Alabama, for the first time and how her four years teaching at Heart of Mary High School impacted her thinking.*

................................................

A group of us, about five sisters, took the train from Chicago to Mobile. The train was called the L&N Hummingbird. We must have come in August, maybe early Au-

*Sister Antonietta (Marilyn Aiello)*

gust, because school would be starting soon. And we were all in the full habit. We got off at the train station, and when the doors opened it was like walking into an oven. Honest to God, it was just that hot. And the parish had sent a parishioner to help us with our baggage. But the parishioner couldn't come into the station because it was segregated. And that was really the first experience I had of segregation. So we had to carry our luggage out of the station so the parishioner could help us. I had grown up in a middle-class, basically Italian-Irish neighborhood on the Chicago northwest side and had never experienced African-Americans. There were no blacks on our side of town or in our schools, and I certainly didn't know anything about segregation. And so that was a shock.

And then we got to Heart of Mary, and that was another shock for me. Heart of Mary was in the middle of a black ghetto. It was the area where African-Americans settled. There was a tremendous amount of poverty. Our convent was surrounded by shacks. I mean real shacks. The school was on the other side of the street from our convent. And the street was not paved! The memory I have is that it was red mud, red clay, because that's what the soil is in Alabama—red clay.

The convent was not air-conditioned. There was a fan, but it was up in the attic. Oh, you were so hot! I mean you'd wake up sticking to the sheets. And the people…like I said, these shacks were all around the convent. And in order to have some air, people lots of times would be up at night. They'd stay up all night, and there'd be all this noise because we'd have our windows open. It was all kind of amazing to me.

Despite all that, I felt very much at home here from the start, and there's a reason I did. I grew up in a very large, emotional Italian family. The family was so important that every Sunday we would go to one grandmother or the other grandmother. You can just imagine. So when I went to Mobile I had never really been exposed to African-American culture, but it was so much like what I grew up with. It was so much like the Italians. You know—outgoing, loving, boisterous, fun-loving, very family oriented. I just totally felt that I fit in. And I don't know, just very well accepted. I mean I never felt shy or that they were somehow evaluating me—whether or not I care about them or like them. I mean I was just accepted. And that's how I felt.

I had very little experience teaching school, but I had a good education and got a lot of mentoring from the sisters who were there. One of the sisters, Patty Caraher, I knew already. We had gone to the same high school in Chicago. She had been teaching in the grade school in Mobile, but the year I came was the year she was assigned to the high school. I was assigned to teach science in the high school. I was the chair of the science department. In fact, I was the only member of the science department!

We wanted the students to be prepared. And we really were willing to go the exta mile. We had a summer program we called Project Opportunity. We would identify students that we felt were college-bound and offer advanced courses. I taught advanced biology. And we taught advanced math, English and writing. Spring Hill College sent Jesuit seminarians to teach, and other sisters would come in the summers too to work in Project Opportunity. The result was we had students accepted at Spring Hill College, at Xavier University in New Orleans, at Howard University in Washington, D.C., and at Midwest colleges such as Rosary, Mundelein and Edgewood. For our students it was not an easy transition, especially those going from the South to the North. As I said, we knew the families. Oh, how we were welcomed into their homes—so many families. And I can still go back there and still be embraced by the people.

..................................................................................................

*As Sister Marilyn becomes more familiar with her new environment, she has to reckon with the reality of segregation, not only in the civic arena but in the church she represents.*

..................................................................................................

When we would go to one of those big events where all the Catholic schools were invited, we couldn't sit with the other high schools; we had to be with the black grade schools. And that was a tremendous shock to me, that the Catholic Church itself was complicit in segregation. The church that I knew, that I felt very much part of, did not show any leadership with regard to this injustice that was taking place. I became more angry as time passed and as I would experience these kinds of things.

The students I had, I can tell you, were very, very motivated, very smart. I don't know how much financial support the families were able to give Heart of Mary. The school did receive money from the Indian and Negro Mission Fund. I'm sure the Josephites made contributions too. As far as the diocese was concerned, I'm not sure if they gave, if they supported us at all. Our Sinsinawa Dominican community gave support; I don't know if we, the sisters staff, received anything in terms of salary.... I have to say it, and it's not a reflection on me, but we did send some of our very best teachers there.

Some students came from the very poor areas of Mobile, and I'm fairly certain they did not pay the full tuition. But many of them came from more affluent families, very good and supportive families. And they came from all over—some from miles and miles away. Their parents would drive them. There was one group of Creoles that lived on an island in the bay, and one of the parents would drive a bus and take all these students to Heart of Mary. Because if they had any African-American blood in them at all, they had to come to Heart of Mary if they wanted a Catholic high school. So we had a whole spectrum of students. Some were very blonde and blue-eyed, some lighter complexioned than I was, and yet they would have to come to Heart of Mary.

......................................................................................

*Sister Marilyn challenges the South's status quo over a fruit fly project.*

......................................................................................

I taught general science, biology, chemistry, physics, and I even taught a college preparatory biology class—advanced biology we called it. And then I had the science club. Which brings me back to the whole segregation thing. The club wanted to do science projects. And I remember two students in particular that did amazing, marvelous projects. One of them was on fruit flies, and our student actually dissected the chromosomes out of fruit flies and produced this marvelous exhibit. Well, I knew that the National Science Institute sponsored regional science fairs for high school students around the country. I discovered that Spring Hill College in Mobile held a charter to sponsor the fair in Mobile. It's a Jesuit college. So I went over to sign my students up. I was told they could not enter, that none of the African-American schools was welcome to enter a project in the fair. Well, I was incensed. It was mind-boggling. I could not accept that.

I went to our superior in the convent and I said, "Sister, I cannot accept this, and I'm going to write the National Science Institute and tell them Spring Hill, a Catholic institution, is practicing segregation by keeping our students from applying. And their charter should be revoked." She said she understood and offered to support me. And she said, "Let me first tell the pastor what you're going to do." And she did. And the pastor called the president of Spring Hill College and whoever was in charge of the science fair. And what do you know, they were all supportive too. I got a letter from the college and they apologized, and they said from now on all African American schools would be welcome! And we were. Well that was the kind of thing that instilled in me and in all of us at Heart of Mary that you had to confront injustice. Otherwise, the system would not change.

Initially, I thought what I was experiencing was the result of decisions made by the local bishop and the local white people. I knew this was racism. But I thought these were individual failings, failings of the bishop, individual failings of the people. Initially, I didn't expand it beyond Mobile or beyond the South. I could see here there was segregation to the point there were separate libraries, separate waiting rooms in the doctors' offices. You knew our children couldn't go to a white hairdresser. Later, I became aware that segregation and racism were rampant in the rest of the country and something important was going on about it. We were living in an historic time.

Sometimes you're not aware of that except when you look back and think about it.

..................................................................................................

**Sister Claretus (Lorraine Rivers Tucker),** *who grew up in Montana, brought her questioning, inquisitive mind to her new assignment.*

..................................................................................................

I'm from Montana, so I had seen only about three black people in my whole life. When I got a call from the motherhouse asking if I would go to Mobile and teach in the high school, I didn't have any concern. I was more thinking about getting there; it was the South and it was late August 1962 and it was very warm and we wearing these big habits in high heat. All that was more on my radar than the kids I'd be teaching.

In the beginning we were speaking two different languages. You know, they had a slow, southern, black accent, and I had this fast northern whatever it was—because it wasn't English to them. *[She laughs.]* So I think that experience, not just the culture and the climate, but the language, helped me. And once I crossed that barrier, or they crossed it—I'm not sure who crossed it—we figured out how to communicate, and luckily it was before school started. I was 25, and I had seniors who were going on 19 or 20, so I was a little intimidated by these guys. But you know, they were wonderful. They were fun to be around. Early on one of the kids asked me if I was prejudiced. I said to him, "I don't know. This is a new experience. If I am, you're going to have to help me to know that." That's just how open they were.

I taught math (basic math, algebra and geometry) and religion. And I did Problems of Democracy for the seniors. That course dealt with basic civics. The students always had a lot of questions about the differences between North and South and how things work politically in Washington. They were wonderfully curious, and several of these guys were thinking of going into the service, so there were a lot of questions about war. And lots of questions about integrating the schools, especially from the underclassmen who were starting at Heart of Mary and knew they probably weren't going to graduate from there. In religion too we had questions and most of them were, "Do you believe that? Do you really believe that?" *[She laughs.]* I was just this naïve person: "Well, that's what the church taught. Of course I believe it." But after you're there for while, and you get a little deeper into things, like the church said slavery was okay and finally figured it wasn't right. So how do we know they got everything else right?

Speaking of questions, I'll never forget the day that Henry Williams, who was teaching across the hall, came over and told me President Kennedy was shot. My first reaction to him was, "That's nothing to joke about." It was so outlandish that it was just unbelievable. All the students heard him say it, and we soon learned it was true. People were asking, "How could that happen?" The memory of the impact it had on the students still flashes by me at times. The basic question they were asking was, "If the president is not safe, are any of us?"

Another thing I remember is the length of time that we were not involved in the civil rights movement. I think when you're in Mobile and you're watching the march on Selma in 1965, and you're seeing all these priests and sisters from around the country in that march, and you're just 100 miles from there, you have to ask yourself the question unless you're practically brain-dead: "Why am I sitting here watching this on television?" Here we are teaching in an all-black school, and the world is fighting for integration. For me, that was frustration.

For a long time the bishop said we couldn't be involved. But that's not a good way to live your life. You really have to know what you believe in, and you have to live what you believe. We believed that integration was the right thing, that black people had a right to education, and they had a right to the best schools and opportunities. They were gifted and generous. They had those rights. I felt it was my responsibility to do what I could to make that happen. After the high school closed, I became very involved in integration and education improvement efforts in Mobile on several fronts.

.................................................................................................

*Father John George Harfmann SSJ arrived at Heart of Mary in 1964, just two years after his ordination as a Josephite priest. His assignment was associate pastor for the parish and religion teacher in the school.*

.................................................................................................

Coming from Brooklyn, New York, and then studying in Washington, D.C., I had never seen face-to-face segregation the way it was in Mobile in those days. The first week I was there, I was sent to help someone at the Mobile Infirmary, which was a little hospital. And when I got there and looked up his name in the registry, I couldn't find it. And when I said his name at the desk, the receptionist said,

*Father John Harfmann (second from left)*

"Is he colored or is the white?" I said, "I think he's Negro." And she said, "Oh well then, he would be in the basement." So I went down to the basement, and that's where I found him. That was my first head-on collision with white and black. It turned out the waiting room for Negroes was outside the building, and they were allowed only in what I would consider wards rather than individual rooms. That was an eye-opener for me, the first of many to come.

I remember my first day teaching at the school. When I came into the cafeteria, one of the seniors, Alexis Herman, was teaching a large body of the students the American Mass music program, written by Father Clarence Rivers. It was probably the first African-American-type music approved in Catholic churches. I got active as a teacher right away in four or five classes a day, all religion. I was there only to help the sisters, who were the major source of teaching at the school, along with a few lay people. It was a tremendous faculty, I mean totally dedicated and giving, providing a lot of activities and opportunities, all pointing to the students toward college. One of my tasks was to interview all the young people and see where we could get them into colleges. I got a lot of leads from the sisters, and the experience was very exciting for me.

I always had an interest in drama, so the first year we did *You Can't Take It With You*. We gathered together every afternoon and put the play together. The second year we decided to go for broke. We decided to do *South Pacific*. So I paid the fees, got the permissions, got the books. We asked one of the students, Diana (Buck) DuBose, to play the piano for it, and that was a challenge because we did a full production. She did magnificently. I mean she went far beyond what she ever thought she could do. In the play we had 44 students. That's 44 out of about 200 in the whole school. We did it, and I have to say we did it almost as Rodgers and Hammerstein wrote it. The play did very well in the community. And we brought it to New Orleans and did it at a Catholic high school.

Then we read about a basketball tournament that goes on each year in Alahambra, Maryland, run by the Knights of Columbus for small schools with fewer than 500 students. Well, our principal, Sister Camelita (McDowell), gave permission, and we collected money in the streets of Mobile in tin cans, buckets and everything else. And we flew the team up to Alahambra for the tournament. Our young people had never played against a white team, never played in front of a white audience. So they didn't do that well playing basketball. But that night there was a talent show, and since they were all in *South Pacific*, they sang the songs from the play, and they won the talent show, so they brought a trophy home anyway. Our people met them at the airport like you would a victorious team. Some of those young people—they're adults now—still remember things like that because it was a step in the right direction. That was really the goal I had in mind—to give these young people the opportunity to see beyond just the building of Heart of Mary.

We got a Head Start program started, thanks to some parishioners who had worked in housing and could give us some details and statistics. No one thought we could pull a proposal together in a short time, but we put it together with the help of the sisters. They taught me what to say, and they made fun of me because I got up and spoke like I was a great educator. But I was really working off little cards they had written on how to teach pre-school children and five-year-olds. But it worked, and we got Head Start based really on what today would be called a Montessori approach. We had play stations and interest corners and lots of activities.

I ran a Christopher leadership program for students some afternoons. I taught how to get up and express yourself. And I said, "You have to learn to do this because down the line you're gonna be in the big picture. It won't just be African-Americans." Integration was the goal, and it was getting closer even in the first years I was there. You know, I stretched myself at Heart of Mary far beyond what I probably should have and challenged them to do the same thing. We all had a lot of chutzpah to do things like *South Pacific*, but we were learning as we went. That was the whole idea.

*February 1967*

From the Back of the Pews to the Head of the Class

# IX. Unexpected Events:
# Stories From Heart of Mary

....................................................................................................

*Unusual happenings and surprises are part of the life of any school, and Heart of Mary was no exception. Here are some memorable events that have stayed with graduates over the years. **Milton Joyner**, a brash teenager, got into real trouble, then redeemed himself following his mother's death.*

....................................................................................................

So I was a little precocious, and I was always liking the girls in the 9th and 10th grades, and I was in the 8th grade. So during the lunch break, I'd be out there talking to the girls, and Sister Bernard (Kelley) would always have to come out and say, "Milton, get back in class." And I'd say, "I'll be with you in a minute, Sister. I'm talking right now." And so Sister Bernard came there one day, and I was out there talking to a young lady I was dating. She was in the 9th grade. Sister said, "Milton!" I said, "I'm talking right now." She grabbed me. I said, "Get your hand away! You don't put your hand on my clothes. You don't buy my clothes!"

And boy, she really went off on me and sent me home, and she told my mother, "He can't come back here. He's expelled." So my mother took my sister out of Heart of Mary. She was in the 10th grade, and she went to Central High, a public school. And she sent me to Mobile County Training School to finish 8th grade, and I transferred to Central for 9th, 10th and 11th grades. Meanwhile, my mother died. And I promised my mother before she passed that I would graduate from Heart of Mary. So I kept my promise, went back there for my last year and finished at Heart of Mary.

*Asked if he harbored any hard feelings toward the school, given the treatment he got from Sister Bernard, Milton launched into a ringing tribute.*

I give Heart of Mary all the credit in the world. I think it did a tremendous job in helping black students like me. I think if it wasn't for that school there and the dedication of the sisters and other teachers, a lot of students would not have excelled to the point that they did. And I think the individualized teaching you got from a small school and the attention that the nuns and priests paid to you, you could not get at the public school. It was a dynamic experience, and I'm grateful I had the opportunity. And having white sisters and priests gave us a sense of not being segregated. You know, here we were interacting with these people, and it gave us a sense of—I don't want to say superiority—but a sense of being as equal as any white guy around. That has stayed with me, especially when I went to the University of South Alabama later and became president of the Black Student Union.

**Paulette Norvel**, *a girl from a poor town, found her outlook suddenly expanding as she encountered an unfamiliar world.*

I'm actually from Mississippi, from Pascagoula, Mississippi, about 39 miles from Mobile. There wasn't a Catholic black high school in our city. My siblings had gone to a Catholic school in Biloxi, Mississippi. They were bused each day from Pascagoula to Biloxi, but by the time I was ready for high school that school had closed. My parents wanted me to have a Catholic school education, so my brother, who was in the seminary at the time, suggested that my parents talk to Gloria Caponis, a woman they knew in Mobile, to see if I might be able to stay with her family and go to Heart of Mary. So that's how it happened. I did not know Mrs. Caponis and I didn't know her daughter Alexis Herman, who was about my own age. So this was a leap of faith for my parents.

My high school experience at Heart of Mary was really life changing. It was a mental and emotional growth period for me. The young people, my peers, were a lot more confident, a lot more articulate than the children I went to school with in Pascagoula, so it forced me to be a lot more like them. In Mississippi we just took things for granted. That's the way things were. I had a very close and probably insular family situation. We went to school, we came home, we went to church, we came home. I didn't go to parties because we were too poor. Nobody had parties. If you had a party it was with your family—cake, ice cream and maybe one gift. But these kids at Heart of Mary were different. Their parents were educated. They had

*Sister Alberta (Patricia) Carahar and Paulette Norvel*

traveled. They held events in their church. The educational experience taught me to think, to do critical thinking, to do analysis, to evaluate situations and circumstances and outcomes in relation to my religious principles. It solidified my moral base and outlook and let me think I could make a difference in the world.

......................................................................................................

*One of the tools Paulette found mind-expanding was the Young Christian Students (YCS) program. It was an American adaptation of the Young Christian Worker approach that originated in Belgium in the 1940s and featured a See-Judge-Act approach. Small groups would analyze particular current events, decide how they conformed or did not conform to basic Gospel teaching, and then decide on an appropriate action to take.*

......................................................................................................

We had these meetings after school, and we began to really look at some of the social injustices in our lives or items we might read in a newspaper, and we talked about what it would take to correct some of the problems we read about. And that really got me thinking. The sisters were always proactive. They gave me role models and examples of what could be done and what our responsibilities were. And we had contact with other

*Class of 1964*

adults like Alexis Herman's father, who was politically active and out in front on a lot of social issues, and like Alexis' uncle, who wrote regularly on issues in the newspaper. So we were surrounded by adults who were educated, informed and responsive.

The issues were usually about racism in accommodations, like hotels and restaurants. I remember once when Alexis' father took a group of us out in a car. His friends, my friends, about six girls, and we were all different complexions, different hair textures, different looks, across the spectrum. He took us to a burger place, and they did not want to serve us. He told them we were international students and asked, "Is this the way you treat an international student? And do you want them to go back to their countries and tell how they were treated?" He went on and on and on. They ended up actually serving us! I was scared and nervous because in Pascagoula my parents would never do anything like that. They might stand up for something, but we wouldn't have gone to a public facility and made a statement. So we got to know people of strong character who would not tolerate any, you know, any enormous disrespect, but at home they probably would have avoided any kind of conflict like that.

Another example, I was pretty good in science, and Sister Marilyn (Antoinetta) encouraged me to enter the science fair at Spring Hill College. I had done a project on the DNA pattern in the eye pigment of a fruit fly. So this was cutting edge stuff at the time, about 1963. DNA was just being spoken about, and we had grown these fruit flies. We cut off their eyes and extracted the pigment. And we did the graduated DNA pattern on a paper, and we also built the molecule. Then Sister Marilyn learned that black children had never been allowed to enter the science fair. So she stood up, threatened to write a letter to someone at the top because these were federal funds that supported the fair. And that could have jeopardized the college's funding.

The university actually backed off, allowing me to participate. And I got third place in the city-wide fair! Sister Marilyn has always contended that the only reason I didn't get first place was because I was black. I don't know that, but that was her contention. She was a science teacher, so she should have known. Of course, we didn't have all the resources that the public schools had. I have a picture of myself in the science lab stirring something in a can. Sister Marilyn did all she could to get us equipment and material. We even had petri dishes, but we improvised a lot. We didn't have the best of anything.

Then there was the time, I think in my sophomore year, that our class went to a Ku Klux Klan rally at the arena in town. They didn't call it the Klan but the White Citizens Council. The announcement said the public could attend and had a right to be there. So the sisters took us, I think in my sophomore year. And the white folks there were throwing things at us, beverage containers and things like that. Oh, we were very calm and quiet. I do remember that, because we'd been coached not to respond, not to react or retaliate. I think we took the experience for granted as part of our education. But I don't remember that I told my parents about it. My mother, of course, would have been very afraid. My father was a bit daring so he would have understood, but mothers always fear for the safety of their kids.

In science, Sister Marilyn was always asking questions and expecting us to answer. She asked why did this happen or why do you think that happened or what do you think needs to be done, and what's the next question? Not so much what's the next answer, but what's the next question. We reacted well to all this because we had a lot of fun with Sister Marilyn—and Sister Patricia (Alberta) too. They were very young, so they were closer to us in age, and they'd be comfortable climbing a tree with us or whatever. They were extremely different than the sisters I had in Pascagoula. I don't know if they were all older but they acted older. They were very conservative, very stiff. We never saw them outside. They were either in school or church. We never went into the convent to see them. I mean we were always students, if that makes sense. We weren't necessarily people. But at Heart of Mary we were Paulette and Alexis and Maryann and whoever. We were individuals. It was an exciting time at Heart of Mary. I learned a lot. Learning has always been exciting to me and it still is.

...........................................................................................................

*Gary Cooper, who would become one of Heart of Mary's most illustrious graduates, talks about a profound, life-enhancing experience early in his school years.*

...........................................................................................................

We lived Down the Bay and I attended St. Peter Claver, but after my seventh grade we lost the nuns. So Daddy got me in Heart of Mary for eighth grade and four years of high school, and I graduated in 1954. I enjoyed Heart of Mary. The nuns had a great influence on us. I especially remember Sister Eulogia (Dawes). She taught math and geometry. She had a poem she used to read to us. It was about segregation and how we should not let it affect us. I don't remember most of it but the last line went, "Remember, there's always room at the top." I've always remembered that line.

Well about ten years later when I was in the Marines, I got assigned as the commanding officer of the Marine detachment of a beautiful new cruiser called the Chicago. It was a job a black man never had before. And in the course of going out to sea, I was sitting in my stateroom and saying to myself, "Are you going to stay in the Marine Corps?" I remembered Sister Eulogia telling me there's always room at the top. So I wrote this note to myself saying, "Cooper, if you're gonna stay, you're gonna be a general one day." I put it in an envelope, sealed it and wrote, "Do not open for 20 years" on the outside. And almost 20 years to that day, the phone rang and it was P.X. Kelley, the commandant of the Marine Corps, and he said, "Gary, I've got good news. You've been selected to become a brigadier general." I got on my knees, and I said, "Thank you, Lord." Yeah! So I have to thank Sister Eulogia too. She was actually one of the nuns we feared. That's probably why she was so damn effective.

....................................................................................................

*Leonard Stiell heard a word of wisdom just in time.*

....................................................................................................

As a freshman I had this math teacher, a lay teacher. At semester exams she thought me and John J. were cheating on the test. So she flunked me. She gave me an F on that test because she said I was cheating. But *[pause]* I'll go to my grave saying I wasn't cheating on that test. So I said, if I'm doing my best and then someone can tell me they gonna flunk me on account of something they think I'm doing, then I'm not really gonna try my best in school. And I didn't. All I wanted to do anyway was play basketball. So I went through high school making Cs and Ds, you know, just enough to pass. And in a way it was a kind of a blessing in disguise, because I had to go to summer school after that first year. I took courses at Central High School, a public school, that were not offered at HOM, like calculus. I actually enjoyed summer school, so I went three summers.

Well, my father knew I could do better than Cs and Ds. He told me that if I didn't do my school work I couldn't play basketball. He worked at the post office from 2:30 to 10:30 p.m. So I played basketball anyway. But he found out. I told him if I couldn't play basketball, I wasn't going to school. In senior year I told Sister Claretus I was going to quit school. We talked about this several times. She asked me, she say, "Do me a favor. Your semester exams are ready to come up." She say, "Do the best you can on the tests just to show me and show yourself how well you could do, how well you could have done if you wanted to."

And I did. I made some pretty scores on those tests. And you know, she told me before I even got my report card how well I did on the tests. She said I should reconsider dropping out of school. She said, "You need to reconsider and stay in school." And I did, and I'm glad I did. So many leaders have come out of Heart of Mary. We've had managers and vice presidents and people high in government and the armed services. I'm not sure I'm educated enough to be a real leader. But I'm somebody who makes himself available. If there's a job to be done and somebody else doesn't want to do it, I'll do it. I've been that way since high school. People ask me how come I've been in charge of the HOM alumni for over ten years? I tell 'em it's because no one else wants the job.

..................................................................................................

*Carol Hill Anderson's* *father discovers a convenient way to beat Jim Crow.*

..................................................................................................

My daddy looked white. He had blue eyes. Now my mama was definitely black. I mean she was a pretty brown, you know like Michelle Obama. You have no doubts in your mind Michelle is a black woman, right? When I was raised, the downtown Mobile area was alive and vibrant and very productive. And right downtown there's the square. It's a little one-square-block park, and then all the stores faced the square. They had a pretty little iron fountain in the square, and they had two pathways going through the park, and they had iron benches down the pathways.

I did not know at the time that black people could not sit on the benches or walk around the square. When I was a little girl my mother would go shopping. And daddy would take us to the square, and he would buy a bag of peanuts and we'd feed the squirrels. And we would play in the square until mama finished. Nobody ever said anything to us, because to look at it, it was my white, blue-eyed daddy out here. He looked white; he looked like anybody's white man. They never said anything to him because they thought of him as a white man out with his half-breed children. He never talked about it as something illegal. I only found out one day when talking to a friend. I said, "Remember when we'd play in the square." And she said, "You did not play in the square." And I said, "Yes, I did." That's when I found out black folks didn't play in the square. But we did.

# X. Archbishop Thomas J. Toolen: Painful Memories

*Thomas Joseph Toolen, a priest of the Archdiocese of Baltimore, Maryland, was named the bishop of Mobile. Alabama, in 1927. He remained bishop, and later archbishop, of Mobile for 42 years—the second longest tenure for a Catholic bishop in U. S. history. He opened many churches, schools and hospitals and spoke often of his concern for black Catholics. But his patronizing references and putdowns of blacks rendered him extremely unpopular in the black and inter-racial community.*

*Especially offensive was the embarrassing position of black participants in the annual Christ the King parade in the late fall. Inaugurated by Toolen in 1931, as an "outward demonstration of Catholic faith," the parade drew crowds of up to10,000, according to Mobile newspapers; the celebration in 1945 at the end of World War II attracted some 20,000. A second yearly Catholic parade and celebration on May Day, honoring the Virgin Mary as Queen of Peace, was added in the early 1940s. At all of these parades, black participants, including the students of black Catholic schools, were traditionally placed at the rear. As a result, the Mass or other events climaxing the celebration were often nearly over by the time they arrived on the scene. For black Catholics, this very "outward demonstration" of their place—not just in society but in their church—remained a continuing source of pain and frustration.*

......................................................................................................

**Aurelia (Bootsie) Taylor Chestang:** Here's a story about the Christ the King parade. In 1956 we marched, and that was the first year Sister Ronald (Thibodeau) was with us. We were the last school in the parade, and by the time we got into Bienville Square, Bishop Toolen *[had finished Mass and]* was giving the benediction. She was furious. And she said to whoever was near her, "Come with me." So about four of us followed her. We got to the bishop just as he was coming down the steps off the platform that was set up in the square. As he was coming down the steps Sister Ronald was coming up to him. He held out his hand for her to kiss the ring. She pushed it aside. She pushed his hand aside. She said, "I'm not here for that!" She said, "You have insulted us. When we got to the square you were giving the final bene-diction. My children are as important as any of these children, as any of these other schools." So she says, "Now next year, if we don't march according to the age of the schools, we're not marching!"

Sister Ronald was very outspoken. She was insulted. Segregation insulted her. I think she felt like when they didn't respect us, they didn't get the respect of the other nuns in the city because they were teaching colored children. And she was not going to let that be the legacy of her work here.

She brought the incident back to Heart of Mary, and she got about five men of the parish to call for a meeting with the bishop. They went down and did talk to him and got it brought up before some kind of a council, and they talked some more. So the next year, 1957, the year I graduated, Heart of Mary was third in line. Third in line!

..................................................................................................

*In fact, in the years after 1957, the Heart of Mary marchers were put back in their traditional last place in line. And that's where they were in 1967 when* **Dora Finley's** *class participated in the march, although the route and Bishop Toolen's role had been altered by then.*

..................................................................................................

We were very fortunate to have this priest early on, Father Vin-cent Warren, because even into my own days, it was known that he would stand up to T.J. Toolen. The bishop would come to Heart of Mary and go, "My poor little colored children." It was like a situation where he was the master, and you know what we were. He was so patronizing toward us.

You were supposed to kiss his ring. He's "Your Excellency," and you get to kiss his ring; it's a privilege. But nobody wanted to kiss his ring because he had done some things to us. My mother tells the story of when they were raising money for Heart of Mary grade school, and they had this thermometer sign in front of the church registering the contributions as they were coming in. And when they got just enough to build this little one-story building, Bishop Toolen took the rest of the money, a good chunk, and built the McGill Institute high school for boys, white boys. And so everyone resented him.

When we had the Christ the King march down Government Street, Heart of Mary was always put at the end of the line. We would march right by the bishop's home, his rectory, and we were told, "Now he will be sitting out on his porch, and when you pass in front of his residence, everybody turn your head to the left and look at the bishop." So one year in my class, we said, "When we get in front of him, we're going to turn our heads to the right." He's gonna look at the back of our heads. And we did it! That's because we had our black consciousness about us by that time.

You know, I don't think any of this damaged our faith. In fact, it helped us in part. We could see two versions of church right in front of our faces. I mean we had the nuns and priests like Father Warren, and they were all on the good side. And then you had this other force at the top, which was primarily Bishop Toolen, on the other side. It was just natural life. You have the good and you have the bad.

...........................................................................................................

**Debra Butler:** I think people were Catholic in spite of the church, particularly black Catholics. I think you had the faith, but I don't think you necessarily respected the church. I think those are really different things. If you believed in the faith and the teachings of the church, then you could be a faithful Catholic without accepting who the church was in Mobile, Alabama. Because the church was very intolerant and very hateful in Mobile, Alabama, but you were sustained by your faith.

Our senior year *[1968]* we did not kiss the bishop's ring. That was our protest at graduation. It was poorly received by the diocese. *[She laughs.]* But we waited until graduation to do it. Bishop Toolen sat in a chair with the dean of education beside him. And we were supposed to get our diploma and kiss the bishop's ring. Instead we just took the diploma and we may have done a little salutatory bow, but we didn't kiss his ring. I think the bishop was stunned. Well, we knew he was closing the school. We were very angry he was closing the school. So what could he do to us? You know, it was a form of defiance, which at 16 feels really, really, really good. And it was also a sort of statement that what he's doing is something really wrong. We're not happy with it. We don't respect you.

...........................................................................................................

*Joyce Cassino:* I did not like him. I knew he was a segregationist. There's no doubt about that, because he endorsed everything that was going on. For a long time I thought I was going to hell because I had this animosity against the archbishop of Mobile. But I did reconcile with that. In fact, when the cathedral did open up *[to blacks]*, I went down into the catacombs where the bishops are buried. I forgave him. I went down there and I put a hand on Toolen's tomb. It was just something I had to do. I…I hated him for so long, I asked for forgiveness, and I forgave him for what he did, keeping us separate and unequal. And we were the church. He was the enemy. He was very powerful. He could have stopped any of the treatment we received. And he did not. Not at all. No!

Yes, I hated him, even as a kid. And I think it's because our parents had such tunnel vision, and they held all these deities on this pedestal, so you could never vocalize anything about your feelings. They're the priests. He's the archbishop. You respect them, you honor them, you almost worship them. And our parents never questioned the separation. This is how they lived, and how we were brought up. So you went to church, and you got in line in the back of that parade.

...........................................................................................................

*Harold DuCloux:* He was for the things he could control. Let's admit it was against the law for black and white kids to go to school together. That's the law, right? He can't break that law. So he has to send us to separate schools. But there's no law about faith and worship. There was no law about the Christ the King parade and always putting all the black schools at the back. In the things he had control over, he didn't make a difference. He chose not to. Growing up, I never liked him. I didn't have the respect for him that I had for our parish priests, some more than others, but I liked and respected them all. Bishop Toolen? Not so much.

My mother was a convert, and she tells the story that she converted because she was a poor black girl growing up in this part of Mobile that was really poor. And there was a Catholic family that lived next door, and when one of the family members died, the priest, white priest, came to their home. So she knew that if there was a religion where white priests would come to a poor black home, that was the religion for her. That's the story she told, and I bring it up because it shows the esteem Catholics were held in by many blacks.

....................................................................................................

**Sheila Flanagan:** He was a very benevolent segregationist and paternalistic for sure. You know how he'd talk about his "good little colored children." He was not a personal hero of mine. But in his time he felt as though he was doing something by making provisions for African-Americans. It was under him that the Blessed Martin De Porres Hospital was built *[completed in 1949]*. And there was a dire need for a place for African-Americans to go, especially black women to have their babies. African-American doctors could not practice at the white hospitals. They would have patients, and if they needed to admit them to the hospital, they would have to get a white physician to take them as patients. So out of that need, Bishop Toolen built Martin De Porres Hospital. And it was a source of great pride in the African-American community, because for the first time there was a new facility where black doctors could actively practice and not have to go through the added bureaucracy of having a white doctor sign off for them.

But he was not really a change agent. He probably did what he thought was best for his colored parishioners, his colored flock. He was not particularly a hero in my family.

*Gary Cooper:* I do know that Daddy registered my brother Billy at McGill *[about 1959]*, and Billy started at McGill. You couldn't tell he was not white. He had kind of blond hair, you know, dark brown. And when they started going through records and they saw that he come from St. Peter Claver *[a black parish]*, guess what? They put him out. Not only did they put him out, Archbishop Toolen was so mad at my dad for trying to integrate the schools that they would not even let him back in a Catholic school. They wouldn't even let him in Heart of Mary. They told him he could go to no Catholic school in the diocese.

Daddy had to send Billy to Detroit to live with my aunt to go to school. Now prior to that time, let me tell you, Daddy said the rosary. We knelt around the bed every night and said the family rosary. Daddy was the most dedicated Catholic you'd ever see. And he ended up committing suicide, my Daddy did. And I am convinced that action *[against Billy]* was what turned Daddy off on the Catholic Church. They wouldn't let him back in any way. And that was Bishop Toolen. He didn't want to integrate the schools then, and he didn't like my daddy challenging him. It was so sad.

*Almost everyone who attended Heart of Mary in the mid-1960s remembers the meeting between Bishop Toolen and Alexis Herman, and they retell the story with pride, though often with variations regarding time, place and other details. Here, **Alexis Herman** herself tells it as though it happened yesterday.*

On a morning in May of my sophomore year, 1963, it was the front-page story in the Mobile *Press-Ledger*: "Area Catholic high schools to march for the crowning of the Blessed Virgin Mary." And they detailed who was in the court and which young lady had gotten picked that year to do the crowning—all the priests, all the clergy, the bishop, big ceremony. So I read the paper that morning. It was one of the things that Sister Patty got us started on—reading the paper in connection with our social justice conversations. My parents were also trying to train us on how to read newspapers, how to pay attention to stories and especially to notice the absence of anything in the black community in the newspapers.

So I'd been practicing what it means to read a newspaper that way, not with much success, but I tried. On this day there it was on the front page: the archbishop, the crowning, the whole bit. And I come on these words: "Area Catholic high schools to march...." And it's like my conscience is so aware of the things we've been talking about in school, and I'm noticing that Heart of Mary is not listed as a Catholic high school in the story, yet all area Catholic high schools participated. So I'm thinking okay, here's an injustice right in the newspaper. This is what we're supposed to be paying attention to, right? So I cut the article out, and I put it in my uniform pocket because we were wearing them to the celebration. And I go as we always did that evening. We line up with our school, we march into Hartwell Field *[the baseball park]*, but I am determined that somehow I am going to ask the bishop why we weren't listed in the newspaper, since we are an area Catholic high school and why we never get to participate in the celebration on the field. We always had to sit in the stands behind the white schools. So I'm trying to think of a way to have this conversation with the archbishop.

We march in, the celebration goes on, they're singing "Hail Holy Queen," the traditional song. We go to our seats, and then I decide that when the bishop is coming off the field I'm going to insert myself in front of him. I'm going to pull out the article and I'm going to ask the questions. I sit through the whole celebration, and when it's almost over I ask my homeroom teacher, Sister Patty (Alberta), if I can be excused to go to the bathroom. I leave the stands and position myself at a spot where I think the recessional of the bishop and clergy is going to pass. But there's this policeman down there kind of guarding the way, and I'm not sure he's going to let me talk to the bishop. I lose my nerve and I don't think I can go through with this. I decide I'll find another day, another time to confront the diocese.

I slip quietly into the dugout and go into the big room under the stands. I plan to hide in there, not knowing this is the room where the bishop and clergy are heading. The door opens and I'm like, Oh, my God! Somebody's coming in here! I hear all these voices and I see this big table draped with this big white tablecloth, and I hide under the table. I didn't know I was in the very room where all these priests would be taking off their vestments and stuff and putting their regular clothes back on. And I'm thinking, no one can know I'm here. This is a problem, a big problem. I decide to wait a while, but then garments start to hit the floor, and I can see them because I'm under the table. So, good Catholic girl that I am, I have a bigger problem: Do I stand and see a room full of naked priests or do I stay under the table? Which sin is greater? But these clothes are still hitting the floor, and I decide I better fess up and get out of here. I decide I have to come out whatever the cost. So that's what I did. I crawl out and I look up. And suddenly there's dead silence in the room—a dead, dead silence. I can see Bishop Toolen, this really, really big man, and he's sitting in a chair. He's got on his black coat and pants. And this priest I knew, Monsignor Bill James, comes over, looks down on me and says, "Alexis Herman, is that you?" And I say, "Yes, Father James, it's me." "What are you doing in here?" he says, and he's starting to look angry. So I run over to Bishop Toolen and I fall on my knees, saying, "I've come to kiss the bishop's ring." I grab the bishop's hand and kiss the ring.

.........................................................................................................

*But Alexis cannot leave well enough alone.*

.........................................................................................................

And just then my courage comes back. I pull the article out of my uniform pocket and I say, "Oh, by the way, Bishop Toolen..." and I just sort of blurt out the whole thing. I'm sure I made no sense. "I want to know why we are never in the procession. Why can't we ever have a representative to crown the Blessed Mother? Why aren't we considered one of the area high schools?" Bishop Toolan is turning red as a beet, and other priests in the room are like, "Alexis, how dare you confront the bishop this way?"

Of course, I'm roundly escorted out of the room. "You go back, find your class and we will deal with this later," they tell me. So of course I got no answers except angry retaliations and how insolent I was, how I had embarrassed them. I go out, and I knew Heart of Mary was always bringing up the tail of the procession, and sure enough, we're bringing up the tail end. We're the last to leave the bleachers. I just kind of fall in line and leave the ball park. My dad brought me and a group of other kids, so we get in the car, we go back home, and I don't tell my parents. I don't tell anybody what I did.

The next day I'm in my homeroom getting ready for class and there's an announcement over the loudspeaker from the principal, Sister Dismas (Slavin); it's blasted all over the school: "Alexis Herman, report to the principal's office immediately." I'm not known as a troublemaker. I'm an activist but not a troublemaker, and I'm a good student. I'd never been called to the principal's office before. Sister Patty, my homeroom teacher, is looking at me. She says, "I think I know what this is all about, but I didn't get the full story." I go to the office and, boy, Sister Dismas, the principal, is mad as the dickens. I mean her arms are folded. I can see her right now. She says, "Tell me you didn't do this. Tell me you didn't embarrass the school this way. Tell me what I've been told you did not do!" So then she tells me she understands I was hiding in the bishop's dressing room and that I confronted the bishop with these ridiculous questions—and how dare you and da, da, da, da. She just wore me out.

And then she expelled me! She said, "You are to go now! You are to get all your books. Clean out your desk and go. You are expelled and I will be in touch with your parents." I'm crying now. I go back to my class, and Patty comes up to me, and I'll never forget it. I'll never forget it as long as I live. Talk about what impacted my life.... It was this one line. Patty looks at me and she puts her arms around me, and she says, "Alexis, you did the right thing."

And to this day, when I talk about what shaped me, it's those words. It was understood I took a big risk. I didn't know it was such a risk at the time. I look back on my life now and I'd say them again. I mean I was validated by Sister Patty. The rest of the story is just kind of history.

I got put out, and I left school. I went to my dad's office. I told him what happened, and his reaction shocked me—totally. He said, "They will not put you out of school for doing what you did! Somebody should have dealt with this a long time ago. It should have been us, as parents." He said, "You go home. I will talk to your mother, but we're going to deal with this."

And what happened was my father organized a group of parents. They went down and confronted the bishop. And that really began a discussion. It was the foundation of what led to the integration of the Catholic schools in the Mobile diocese. They negotiated about what needed to happen right away. And the following year Bishop Toolan gave the directive that all area high schools were going to be integrated. We had our first two trial students, as we called them, going to the white school. That year too Heart of Mary marched in the parade at Hartwell Field, and we weren't last in line. I was a junior that year, and it's always a senior who crowns the Blessed Virgin. Marie Delage, a senior, was the first ever from Heart of Mary to have that honor. It's kind of funny I'm telling this story. I haven't told it in years. I don't know where Marie Delage is, but she was the first. Obviously, I got reinstated in school and graduated in 1965. Patty really made a singular difference in my life at that point. She really did. She didn't put me down. She helped the rebel in my heart.

...........................................................................................

*Years later, when Alexis attended college in the North, she faced a crisis of faith.*

...........................................................................................

The church preached the gospel of inclusion and justice, but it really wasn't about that. The church was just as segregated as all other institutions, and so I stopped going to Mass. I decided the church was hypocritical. I stopped participating in any of the school social events. Eventually, I left the school. I'm angry at the church. I'm done. I come home, and I actually end up at Spring Hill College for a semester while I'm home. I take a course from Father Albert Foley (SJ). One evening we're having this conversation and we get into this whole debate about institution and race and religion. It was a big, big deal for me. I didn't know it at the time, but as I look back on it now, I know that a seed got planted. I had put too much into the church in terms of its human makeup. My faith, my belief was fallible, and the individuals of the church were just as fallible. What my faith should be about was walking in the Spirit of our Lord and Savior Jesus Christ. And not everybody walked that walk.

It was a big idea for a young woman at the time, and I had a difficult time putting it all together. I started to heal in terms of not being angry with God and not being angry with the church. I was able to understand that human beings in the body of Christ are fallible, and you can make a decision to work inside the body of Christ or you can choose to remove yourself. Over time that decision has been a defining moment for me.

*Archbishop Thomas J. Toolen, 1966*

*Sister Ricarda Bronson OP, with (from left) Joan Hall, Sheila Anthony,
Cecil Simpson, and Cordell Lang, all students in the 1960s*

# XI. Desegregation: The Unraveling Begins, 1964-1967

*Although the civil rights movement had been gaining momentum throughout the South since the late 1950s, there was little public discussion, much less agitation, in Mobile. But when four black girls died in the Klan bombing of a Baptist church in Birmingham, Alabama,, in 1963, only 250 miles from Mobile, it was clear to both civil and religious leaders that the movement would eventually be coming to town. Bishop Toolen broke his customary silence, condemning the bombing as a "shameful act," and said he could not believe that a "civilized human being" could hate another because of that person's color. Any Catholics with such leanings "should pluck this hatred out of their hearts and recall that all men are created equal," he said.*

*The next year, in April 1964, he surprised friend and foe alike by announcing the integration of Mobile's Catholic schools: "After much prayer, consultation and advice, we have decided to integrate all the schools of the diocese. I know this will not meet with the approval of many of our people, but in justice and charity this must be done." However, decisions about accepting new students would be left to principals, pastors and school boards, he said, leaving wide latitude for compliance. Less than a month after endorsing integration, Toolen, speaking to the Friendly Sons of St. Patrick organization, reverted to his usual message when civil rights were discussed. He denounced "crusaders who see integration as a holy cause," adding that "sane and sensible Negroes realize we are trying to bring them up to the standards they should have."*

*Integration of the schools would prove to be a very, very gradual process. Even more gradual would be the realization that Heart of Mary High School would not survive. Response to the coming of integration varied widely among Heart of Mary students.* **Harold DuCloux** *and* **Joyce Cassino***, for example, had completely opposite reactions. But neither was ready to go elsewhere, and neither had to, since both graduated before Heart of Mary High School closed.*

*Harold:* I wasn't ready. The nuns hadn't been talking about it at all—not until much later when the protests really got going and they changed to civilian clothes. It was as if they let the hounds out, so to speak.

*Joyce:* We had one lay teacher, Mr. Williams, and I do remember him in our religion classes talking about the movement. But for me it was just an individual initiative. I can remember the early marches, and we talked about that.

*Harold:* Yeah, the Selma to Montgomery March or even the "I Have a Dream" speech. I totally don't remember being aware of any of it at the time.

*Joyce:* I was wishing I was there. I remember watching TV and saying, "I need to be there." I had a sense of already being a part of this movement. I don't know if this was because I was confident enough and I was ready to go out and tackle this brave new world. I just had this sense of confidence that this was a very good thing that was about to happen. It was scary but still exciting. I knew I was going to be able to use all those skills I had learned. I had the edge. So there was a club at Toolen, the Catholic Youth Organization (CYO). I went over there and joined, and at the first meeting I remember taking charge of the meeting. That social work capacity was already in me. But there was not a good reception. I found out the Toolen girls were not the prim white girls I always thought they were. I became aware of their shortcomings, and that was a revelation. Both Harold and I were asked in 1965 *[to leave Heart of Mary]* to integrate the white schools, as a step toward full integration. I declined. I had been at Heart of Mary 11 years and I wanted to graduate from there. I was upset and angry because they had handpicked the ones they wanted to go and integrate the schools. We were told to go home and talk to our parents about it. I made a spontaneous decision. When I went home my parents left the decision up to me. I said no.

*Harold:* Yeah, I declined too. My reason was more gutteral. I was playing football for Heart of Mary at the time, and I knew I couldn't play football for the white school. McGill may have been a bigger school and have been better—in quotation marks. But as far as I was concerned, there was no academic advantage because I was prepared to go to college, so it didn't matter where I graduated from. So why should I leave my social network to go and be immersed in this place where people did not want me? I said no.

*Joyce:* I still felt the movement was important and I had an obligation to help it along. The Head Start program was just beginning. I volunteered and remember going into central city neighborhoods and putting flyers on doors about the program, and I started going to civil rights meetings. A lot of these kinds of activities were spearheaded by Alexis Herman, who was two years ahead of me at Heart of Mary. She was quiet and assuming but a natural leader, and she became a kind of mentor for me.

*Harold:* You should understand that in the South the civil rights movement was not front page. And the African-American community in the South in general did not support the civil rights movement physically. They wanted the change, but our parents were not participants in the change. So when people like the Freedom Riders started coming into towns as catalysts for change and bubbling over with enthusiasm, people in those towns were going, "When you guys leave, we're going to have to live with this."

...................................................................................................

*Another who declined an invitation to transfer to a white school was* **Marion Lewis**.

...................................................................................................

Things were starting to happen with integration. My senior year, 1964-1965, two students from Heart of Mary went to integrate McGill Institute. That was the first time we ever had students at a white school. I guess the bishop was working with the pastors and telling them, "We need some black students to go to McGill, the boys' school, and Bishop Toolen, the girls' school." John Finley was one of them who went. His father owned a couple pharmacies in Mobile. Once a year we had vocation day, and Heart of Mary seniors would go to either McGill or Toolen. Of course all the whites would be in one area and we in the other. And I remember that particular vocation day because we looked over at the other side, and we saw a couple dark-skinned people sitting amid the white folk. And we said, "There they are."

........................................................................................

*Carol Hill Anderson tried to socialize with Toolen students, as recommended by her teachers, but found it an unrewarding task. She opted to stay at Heart of Mary.*

........................................................................................

The nuns knew they were getting ready to close Heart of Mary, and I can't remember when they broke the news, but they were urging some students to go to McGill and Toolen when I was a freshman in 1964. I wanted to integrate. You know, let's go for it. I want to go to Toolen. My mother wouldn't let me go. And I said, "Why? I want to integrate." My whole thing was, "I want to go there." And my mother's whole thing was, "I want you to enjoy your high school years, and I know Heart of Mary is going to give you an education."

What I later found out was that the kids who were the first wave *[those who went to the white schools voluntarily in the mid-1960s]* were isolated, they were not taught, they had a terrible time. Girl, they walked through the shadow of the valley of death. So I stayed at Heart of Mary, and I am so glad my mother wouldn't let me go to Toolen.

During my years at Heart of Mary, there were efforts made to mix us with the students from the white schools. We would go over to Toolen and have Mass together, and some girls from Toolen came over to us and tried to have a conversation. They tried to. We didn't go to each other's dances or anything, but they tried to mix us together. But it didn't work. They were all failures, because we didn't socialize. We just looked at them. They looked at us. Somebody would try to get a group discussion started, and it just flopped. I didn't have any interaction with white people until I went to Heart of Mary, and I forgot the nuns were white. When somebody would talk about "those white nuns at Heart of Mary," it would always kind of jerk me, and I'd have to think, oh yeah they are white. It's as if they had become black. So we had no experience before relating to ordinary white people.

........................................................................................................

*Early integration efforts were a problem for **Debra Butler** too. She chose to remain at Heart of Mary.*

........................................................................................................

We started in my sophomore year, 1965-1966, doing activities with Toolen. The diocesan education board made the effort. There was a series of competitive one-act plays between the schools and opportunities to interact socially. It was very strange because Toolen wasn't very comfortable with it. I can remember one time going there and having no one speak to me. Not the faculty, not the nuns, not the students, and I don't know whether they were afraid of us or whether they just didn't like us. We were of course well behaved and well groomed and all that, but no interaction. I know the black students that did go to the white schools there were pretty isolated. My brother who went to McGill four years later got in fights every day. My brother who went eight years later had a more normal experience.

You have to remember there was very little interaction of any kind in our communities. And it's really strange because in Mobile you have white and black neighborhoods that were next to each other. And I can remember as a child playing with white kids, but that only occurred until you were maybe ten, and then they withdrew. You could play in creeks and streams and build lean-tos in the woods and do all sorts of exploring, and it was pretty safe. But after nine or ten that just didn't happen anymore.

*Patricia Kelly Lofton shares the pros and cons of having to leave Heart of Mary and complete her high school education at a white school.*

I went to Heart of Mary from first grade through second year high school when the school was closed down. I felt I had a good education, and that was confirmed in 1968 when I went to Toolen for my junior and senior years. We were in some of the top classes over there. We went there with basic skills. We fit in because at every level we participated and we did well. So I think the unrest wasn't the same as it was in some places. I don't think the teacher problem was serious either. I think they were ready for us. I could see an effort had been made, that the faculty had been prepared. Somebody had prepared them, because the transition was as smooth as it possibly could have been. I saw nothing but excellent teaching, and I decided that's what I wanted to do.

We didn't want to go to Toolen. Of course we didn't want to go. We wanted to stay at Heart of Mary and finish. But they had said, "This is it!" Yes, I did miss Heart of Mary because we had a culture that most programs didn't have. We had plays where the children would perform, like *Porgy and Bess*, a lot of oratorical speaking. People don't realize that a lot of black schools had those kinds of things. I participated in those cultural arts. We didn't have those at that time at Toolen. So something important was lost.

Still, with times changing, integration probably was needed. We needed to have equal footing. Small high schools weren't getting the money they needed to do a good job. Integration is also good because it can change perceptions. After graduation I went to South Alabama College, earned a degree in elementary education and had a job before I left school. I taught first grade at Baker, a K-12 school up by the airport. I knew the parents were concerned since they always had white teachers over there. And the first year I know they were looking at me cautiously. But I didn't experience problems. I was one of those gung-ho, take-charge teachers. And in the second year they all wanted their children in my classroom.

*Sheila Flanagan makes a case for the advantages of desegregated education, but in the end, she states her verdict.*

The transition from Heart of Mary closing and my class going to Bishop Toolen was billed as something positive, something that was going to be great for us. Heart of Mary was very limited in resources. And it was sold to the students and parents that going to McGill and Toolen would be a good thing. But in hindsight I do realize the special nurturing we received at Heart of Mary was something we did not get at McGill or Toolen. My feelings are that we became a problem because they had to adjust the school for us and weren't thinking about the adjustment we were having to make to go to those schools. And I don't know whether we were really prepared for what we would experience, because there was a natural resistance—not only because of the racial component but because we were another school merging into an already established school. So naturally there was friction. When Heart of Mary closed, you know, these schools got this big transfusion of the African-American culture all at one time. So it was interesting. *[She laughs.]* Of course, the classes were much larger at Toolen. In fact the school was so overcrowded that we were on double sessions at times. Some kids would go to school from 7:00 a.m to noon, and then some would come at 12:30 and go until 4:00 p.m. It was a mess.

I felt the teachers we had at Heart of Mary were excellent because they were nurturers and wanted to make sure we got the best education. Nothing was lacking as far as instruction was concerned. Maybe we were lacking in equipment and facilities in the building, but you know, some kids came from very humble backgrounds and excelled beyond anybody's imagination. I do know that after our first year at Toolen, we all gathered in the auditorium, and someone would go and put a hand on the shoulder of each student admitted to the National Honor Society. And this first year, there were more kids from Heart of Mary selected for the society than from the rest of the school! There were very bright students that went to Heart of Mary, and the teachers prepared us well. I remember that distinctly and with a lot of pride. We made our mark. And I think from then on the Toolen people still didn't accept us, but they had to respect us. And our girls almost took over the volleyball team because they were so good at it.

But I recognize that the transition from an all-black to an all-white school has a lot of trauma associated with it. It was hard. When you're a teenager that's what you're always working for, trying to be accepted by your peers. It was especially hard when your peers are an already established class that is all white and really doesn't want you there. I remember when the advertisement came out about the Azalea Trail Girl program. They were keeping it a secret because they didn't want any black girls in on it. But somebody in the office informed the black girls, and so many of us applied. I don't think that year they even had a white girl from Toolen go. And that first year we weren't even invited to the girls' annual Christmas party. We raised our own money and had our own party. But unlike what they did, we did invite some of them. We had some episodes and skirmishes at Toolen I'll never forget. One girl got up on a table in the lobby where a huge portrait of Bishop Toolen was hanging and proceeded to deface it with a magic marker between classes. No, the transition didn't go as smoothly as some people may have thought.

Looking back, I wish the fight had been fought to keep Heart of Mary open. But I don't think that was an option. And the thing that softened the blow was the closing of the Convent of Mercy (High School) too. It wasn't just the black schools they were closing, and that made it easier for people to accept the decision. And I'll say I had at Toolen one of the best history teachers I ever met. But I think toward the end of my junior year I realized that going to the new school wasn't a better thing for me. I realized I had left the best place.

*Dora Finley recalls the rough-and-ready days she experienced at Toolen after Heart of Mary closed.*

My cousin John Finley was the first black to graduate from McGill Institute. That was in '66. He had a horrible experience because he was the only black child there when he went over. Nobody talked to him, and it left a bad mark on him that he carries to this day. And there was a black girl who was the first to graduate from Toolen. But after they closed Heart of Mary after the last graduation, in 1968, I was among the black people who came en masse to the two white schools. And there was chaos when we got there. The students attitude was, "You are not coming here and taking over our school." So the first day we were there we saw a black girl we knew, Lynette Gail. She had been with us every year at Heart of Mary through eighth grade, but her mother had sent her to Toolen for high school, as part of the early integration. Lynette was standing in the hall, and these white girls were throwing her books on the floor and stomping on them. I said, "What y'all doing?" It came out that Lynette had told them she was Spanish, and when they found out she was really black they turned on her. So I said, "Uh, you're gonna pick those damn books up now." *[She laughs.]* We had a whole group from Heart of Mary with us at the time. I said, "We're the United States Action Movement, and we're not taking no stuff like that!" It was the first time we had met with challenge. Yeah, they picked up the books. But it was a constant struggle, every day. It was one argument, one thing, after another.

I know integration was something that needed to be done But it completely ruined school for me. Everything was a fight. To get the first black cheerleader we formed the African-American Service club, so we got a representative on the student council. We bloc voted for me to be Miss United Fund. But none of it was a fun experience like I had at Heart of Mary. That was a good, well rounded experience, where you were surrounded by people that loved you and that you loved.

*Jerry Pogue, holding the American flag, leads a local march
after the assassination of Martin Luther King Jr.*

# XII. A Time of Upheaval: The Movement in Mobile, 1968

*1968 was a year of tremendous consequence and change in Mobile. The assassination of Martin Luther King on April 4th was a kind of seismic shock sending reverberations in all directions.*

- *Within a week, on April 7th, the civil rights movement arrived in the city and was holding its first march.*
- *On May 24th Archbishop Toolen gave permission for priests and nuns to participate in demonstrations.*
- *And on May 26th Heart of Mary High School held its final graduation ceremony. By Labor Day the school's staff had moved on to new challenges.*

*The decision to close the school appears to have been made in late 1966, when the general counsel for the Sinsinawa Dominican order met with Archbishop Toolen and the superintendent of the Mobile Catholic schools. The reasons for closure included the high school's financial drain on the parish and especially the need to support desegregated education in Mobile. There was also the belief that desegregation would not result in more than a handful of white students coming to Heart of Mary at best. It was determined at the meeting that the 1967-1968 school year would be HOM High School's final year. The grammar school would continue operation*

*In a letter to the clergy, Toolen said priests and nuns could take part in public civil rights demonstrations, provided their presence is "just, legal and in no way conducive to violence, by fomenting or condoning disrespect for law and order." Participation, he said, would be only "on an individual basis and not in the name of the church." No one, he added, could speak for the church without his permission.*

*Civil rights action in Mobile was carried out largely by a home-grown organization called the Neighborhood Organized Workers, better known as NOW. For most of its existence, NOW held its weekly meetings in the Heart of Mary school cafeteria, with the cooperation of local nuns and priests. The organization's president was Noble Beasley; vice president was James Finley, a Mobile pharmacist and father of Dora Finley.*

.......................................................................................

**Fred Richardson**, *the NOW treasurer, who was not a member of Heart of Mary, was interviewed for this book and talked about NOW's activities and its close, supportive relationship with Heart of Mary.*

.......................................................................................

It wasn't until the death of Dr. Martin Luther King that I felt compelled to do something. And what happened is we tried to commemorate Dr. King's death with a memorial. We put in for a permit to march down to the auditorium to make some speeches about our fallen leader. The city fathers said, "No." Because if we did, according to them, it may break out into a riot. People had rioted all over the nation, and a march might cause people to riot here. We said, "We need to march anyway. We can't let a man such as Dr. King die and we don't whisper a word." So, we went and marched on April 7, 1968, just three days after King's death. We marched, made speeches, and had police officers everywhere, as though we were common criminals. After that, a group of us met, and we came to this conclusion: If not now, when? If not us, who? It is not going to get any better unless we take a stand and make it better.

The Neighborhood Organized Workers (NOW) was born out of this meeting. We chose us a leader, picked a board of directors. I was put on the board of directors and made the treasurer of the organization. And at that point then, I had to give up thinking about myself. What if I get killed? I had to let that go. I just had to let that go. And my point is that whatever might happen to my life, I've got to do this. Now today, I wouldn't do that. *[He laughs.]* No, I wouldn't do that today. But then, we just had to do something. But when we set out to hold meetings to organize the community, we found ourselves closed out, because the churches wouldn't let us in.

We went to almost all of the major churches in the city, True Vine, the Stone Street Baptist Church and Mount Zion, asking to hold meetings there, and you know, those pastors were fearful that something harmful would happen to them if they allowed us to do that. They didn't want to be associated with the movement for fear of retaliation. B.D. Lambert, pastor of True Vine Baptist Church, was also the pastor of the church in Montgomery, side by side with Dr. King. And Dr. King asked him to get the ministers here to allow him to bring the movement to Mobile. And they said "No, we don't need him here. Tell him not to come." It was based on fear that the white community would rebel against us if we bring such a man as Dr. King in our city. Fear had engulfed a lot of people we thought were real strong; they caved in from the pressure of those people in charge of our city.

Well, we found a home at the Most Pure Heart of Mary, a most unlikely home. It was the most unlikely home in that many of the students at that school were from families whose skin was light. You know, the darkest skinned kids had to go somewhere else. At least that's what some people thought. But Heart of Mary allowed us to come, no matter what the color. They lowered the bar. And they said everybody can come in here. So, once a week we held our meeting. We had standing room only, and this happened from 1968 to 1974. And I'll tell you, go to any city and find a movement that lasted that long.

As if making up for lost time, NOW launched an intensive campaign of action: picketing school board meetings, declaring a boycott of white-owned businesses that refused to hire black employees, encouraging marches and demonstrations by neighborhood and local citizen groups, and even publishing their own newspaper.

We met at Heart of Mary year after year after year. Those sisters dedicated themselves to the movement, and I take my hat off to them, but I also take my hat off to Most Pure Heart of Mary school, because we met in the cafeteria every week, and no matter what Bishop Toolen was saying, they did not change. They didn't. We continued to meet. Evidently, they saw the movement to be of a greater importance than any instruction the bishop gave to them.

One reason we had so many people at our meetings was because on certain nights people would show up with issues and tell us about them. We had a time period set aside for them to come forward, and they'd say, "I was working at such-and-such a place, and they fired me," and this, that and the other. "They wouldn't let me in because I was black." We took all of those issues down, and then next week we reported on what we did about those issues. And the place would be jammed, packed. Normally we would get a minister from somewhere to come and give us some spiritual guidance. We couldn't come into their church, but they would come here. Oftentimes we couldn't come into their church because the members didn't want us in there. Some of those pastors probably would have allowed us to come, but the members were afraid. They had to go to work, and they didn't want nothing to come up against them. But at Heart of Mary, we had committees and each one would give a report: a bread basket committee, a transportation committee, handbill committee, newspaper committee. We had our own newspaper. Everybody would come and give their various reports on what was happening. All of our meetings were very interesting.

The people came from a cross-section of all of our citizens. They were not people just trying to gain something from being there. We had people that had a lot to lose in coming out to those meetings. And if you look at the members of our board, almost everyone on there had a degree from somewhere, almost all of them. And many of them were schoolteachers. They had a lot to lose. I was with the postal service. Surely, I had a lot to lose. But we didn't let that stop us from doing what we were compelled to do.

...............................................................................................

**Debra Butler**, *a member of Heart of Mary's last graduating class, comments on the artificial calm imposed by the city fathers.*

...............................................................................................

The politicians in Mobile were very crafty, actually, in keeping a lid on this whole notion of disenfranchisement and anger. They selected a group of people who were a sort of an insulation between the masses of folk who were really pissed off and the white community, in order to keep things calm. They said basically, "We don't want to be like Selma or Birmingham. We're better than that. We can work out our differences." And that sort of collusion kept an outward calm. There was no catharsis. There was no way and no need, they believed, to have the kind of truth and reconciliation efforts they had in South Africa. None of that happened in Mobile.

So there was a lot of simmering resentment that just wasn't dealt with. In the long run, I think, it hindered Mobile more than it helped. Birmingham was able to get it out, get it done and move on. And that city is twice as big and twice as prosperous as Mobile. This insular group kept a kind of lid on a lot of the resentment. And a lot of it still hasn't been dealt with.

......................................................................................................

*Pamela Donald Hutchinson, also a graduate in the final class at Heart of May, tells about her early civil rights activities.*

......................................................................................................

After Martin Luther King's death, the nuns got involved in the movement, but they did not openly get us involved. We talked about the marches and all in the classroom as part of current events. Then there would come an announcement on a day that school would close down at 1:30 or whenever "because there's going to be a march on Davis Avenue, and we want you all to get home and be safe before the march starts." And then the sisters would put on their Darth Vader capes, and we'd see them coming out. And we'd be like, "Hey, where y'all going." They'd admit they were going to the march, but they would never look back and say, "You all come with us." They would be on their own, and sometimes we'd be like mice following the Pied Piper.

I remember one time, instead of going to my aunt's house like I was supposed to if school was out, me and some of my friends got in the march and went on downtown. Now my parents had told me specifically, "Do not go! Don't you get involved!" And this day we followed the sisters all the way. They gave us all kinds of instructions what to do if horses started running over us, and if they come at us with billy clubs, and if they start shooting tear gas. They were telling the guys how to protect the women, how to get in a fetal position. I remember being scared but caught up in the moment. Anyway, the march stopped, and somebody read something about a change in schedule and trouble with getting the parade permit, and all of a sudden the march was disbanded.

So I was able to hurry up and get home before my folks came home from work, and I was doing my homework when they came in. But they watched the news every night, and the TV news comes on. And the camera shows the march. And who do they see out there front and center with her little uniform skirt on? So I was punished for that. They got me. But I realized now it wasn't that they were against it. They were afraid. They were afraid for me, and they were afraid for the sisters. We know now the Mobile police undercover people were out there taking pictures and investigating the people who were involved. You know what I'm saying. I knew Sister Claretus (Lorraine Rivers Tucker) would be out there, and I remember Sister John Baptist (McCarthy), and I know Sister Marilyn (Aiello) and Sister Patty (Caraher) were really involved.

After Dr. King was killed, the city comes together all of a sudden and has this program at the civic center downtown. And the ministers and priests are sitting on the stage. And this woman just walks up to the mic, and she says, "Let me tell you why Martin Luther King never came to the city of Mobile. They didn't want him here." So she starts going on and on, telling everything. Some priest jumped up and told the choir to start singing; they tried to drown her out. People started protesting, "Let her speak! Let her speak!" So that just disrupted the thing altogether. You had all these ministers, all these city leaders up there, professing to be all about Dr. King and what he was teaching. And when he wanted to come, they wouldn't let him in the city. And that woman was telling it, but they didn't want to hear it.

When I was in school, I thought the Catholic Church was in our corner because we knew people like Sister Claretus and Sister Marilyn and Father (John) Harfmann (SSJ). I thought maybe all Catholics thought that way. So I've been struggling with that ever since. It's not about my faith in God but about the institution of the church. I have some issues. I struggle. I really do.

*Sister Claretus (Lorraine Rivers Tucker) taught in the school until it closed, then worked part time with NOW and the Mobile archdiocese.*

W e marched. We did it with the people in the area so that they were safe. After we closed the school in 1968, I worked part time for the diocese in religious education in the black parishes out in rural areas and part time in the office of the Neighborhood Organized Workers (NOW). And one of the things I did for NOW was establish after-school programs in reading and math. In Trinity Gardens we had a really big group, but we were also in several places in Mobile where kids would go after school. And the sisters and some of the lay teachers from Toolen-McGill helped out, and so did some of the students from Spring Hill College. My job was to establish these programs and find the people to work with them. But it became a network for when there were marches. We had this whole group of people we knew were civil rights supporters, and they helped with civil rights actions.

We also had a program for high school dropouts. One example was a kid who needed to get a driver's license to work at a delivery job; he needed to learn to read so he could read street signs. An Irish sister in one of the grade schools became his tutor, and she taught him how to read and how to pass the driving exam; she even went with him when he took the exam. We really reached out to a broad band of people. And since I was at Heart of Mary and our NOW meetings were at Heart of Mary, I was a person these people from all over got to know.

It was exciting to be able to do these things—another way besides our school that we were able to help people. It was just the right place to be. I never imagined I'd be doing this kind of work, and I wasn't really afraid. But I do remember the first time we were trained to protect ourselves. You know, what do you do if the cops come along with their batons and are going to crack you on the head. I thought, "Wow! More dangerous than I imagined." But when we marched and when we went to jail or whatever, it was all part of what we were supposed to do.

*A devoted supporter of NOW, **Father William James** acted as an informal chaplain.*

*Father William James*

The difficulty was there were a few people who called themselves a kind of committee on race. That wasn't their real title, but it included the mayor, some other city officials and a few leaders of the black community. What they mainly did was keep Martin Luther King out of Mobile. And they did not respond in any way to the death of King.

So when NOW got organized, the Heart of Mary sisters became part of an important group that included some Jesuit and Josephite priests, some scholastics from Spring Hill and some really powerful people in Mobile. We had a lot of marches, and we had Friday night meetings that would fill the Heart of Mary cafeteria. My job was to say some prayers before the meeting. I remember Sister Maureen Kelley and Maureen Kennedy, Nora Ryan, Rosetta Brown and Marilyn Aiello. There were a lot more, but my memory doesn't go back that well.

In those days we had just had the Second Vatican Council, which I've always said was the number one of the 21 church councils during the 2,000 years of the church. And I was on fire to try to help the black community in the small parish where I was, St. Francis Xavier in Toulminville. The church *[which became a kind of gathering place for activist Catholics in the late 1960s]* would be full every Sunday with black and white people. It was the most integrated situation in Mobile. Some of the Heart of Mary sisters were always there and some nuns from St. Peter Claver and other convents in Mobile. The sisters were the leaders in trying to reshape opportunities through education in the Mobile community. Without the nuns, I would have failed any attempts I tried to do. You know, women have a tendency to bring out the best in men.

......................................................................................................

*Carol Hill Anderson recounts her frustration when she overslept and missed a tear-gas episode at an early demonstration.*

......................................................................................................

Most of the Heart of Mary kids got involved in the civil rights movement, most of them, not all. It just depended on your parents. We all went to the meetings. We knew who Martin Luther King was and we all knew what he was about. But this was Mobile. You could get killed…. But I wanted to be involved. I remember wanting to go to a demonstration over in Prichard. It's a small city and very red-necked, very racist. But I was really tired and knocked out from teaching Bible school at Heart of Mary. So I told Mama to wake me the next morning so I could go to the demonstration. I had gone to demonstrations before, and Mama would pick me up and pick up folks and take them to vote and all that.

Well, she did not wake me up! And I was so mad because it turned out that was a day everybody got thrown in the paddy wagon and they shot tear-gas up into the paddy wagon. Oh, I missed it! And all my friends—Shirley who went to Heart of Mary with me—had gotten tear-gassed. And when they asked me where I was, what did I say? I was taking a nap? I was so mad I didn't get tear-gassed. [*She laughs.*] Don't you know my Mama didn't wake me up on purpose? Don't you know she knew what was gonna go down in Prichard that day? And it was so embarrassing. I didn't come because I was taking a nap. I was tired.

Another time my boyfriend Raymond and I went with a big crowd, mostly high school students, and we sort of took over the steps of the Mobile courthouse. The National Guard was lined up across the street from us—with guns. And the next thing I know, here's my mother coming up behind the National Guard, and she's talking to one of them who's holding a flag. And here we were, all on the courthouse steps in a kind of standoff with the National Guard. Somehow, I don't know how, my mother ended up behind the line of soldiers talking to this man with the flag. Then some of the leaders of the march crossed the street, and they all had a conversation with the man with the flag. He was obviously the captain or colonel or whoever. Well, we sang "We Shall Overcome," and after we finished they disbanded us, and we all kind of went home. I never understood what had happened, but I think with my mother going behind the line and the leaders of the march going over and talking, it had gotten to the point that people didn't know what to do. You know, how do you save face? So it was all over.

Looking back, this was in a way a Heart of Mary event—lots of students from our school, their friends from public schools, people who had dropped out of Heart of Mary, not because of grades but because of poor economics.

# XIII. Climax:
# Protest and Arrests, 1969

*NOW's most ambitious action was a planned picketing of America's Junior Miss Pageant, a nationally televised, yearly event proudly held downtown at the Mobile Municipal Auditorium. It was scheduled for May 1-3, 1969. From the beginning, gross employment inequality in local government had been a target of NOW's complaints and the theme of demonstrations. NOW wanted the city to hire a black assistant manager for the auditorium as a move in the right direction and as a signal to the city's business establishment still virtually devoid of black employees at administrative levels. The pageant was sacred to city fathers, not just for the revenue it provided, but for boosting the image of Mobile as more than a stop on the way to New Orleans. It was not likely they would take kindly to picketing or any other effort to disrupt the city's moment in the sun. So far civil rights demonstrations had proceeded without incident. NOW reasoned that law enforcement would show its tough side in this case, perhaps even triggering a severe crackdown on activists. **Sister Marilyn (Antonietta) Aiello** and others from Heart of Mary decided to view the action, not as picketers but as supporters across the street.*

...................................................................................................

One of our sisters, Rosetta Marie Brown, had been at the NOW meeting when the decision was made about picketing the auditorium during the Junior Miss Pageant. She asked us at the convent if it would be okay if she was one of the picketers on the first night of the pageant. We said yeah, that sounds all right. Picketing is legal if you follow certain rules, so we didn't feel she would be in any danger. She then asked if the rest of us would come and support the picketers by standing in this little park that was right across the street from the auditorium, in view of the picketers and the auditorium entrance. We said yes, we could go there and stand in support. There were about ten or eleven of us living together at that point, so we would have two carloads.

I went in the first car with four or five others *[including Sister Patty (Alberta) Caraher and Sister Claretus (Lorraine Rivers Tucker)]*. As we left Heart of Mary, we noticed a car parked on Davis Avenue with white men sitting in the car. We thought it was strange and figured it was the police or maybe the FBI. Well, we kept going and decided not to park at the auditorium, because there was a big traffic jam. But right across the street on Government Street was the bishop's house and the diocesan offices. We decided to park in the diocesan office lot because we could get in and out easily over there. Then we all got out, crossed the street and walked into the little park.

And here was this policeman standing there as if he was waiting for us, "You can't stay here," he said. "I want you to walk along the sidewalk and go back where you came from." We were a little confounded, but we thought that's what we'll have to do. We started back to our car, and we didn't get very far. A bus pulled up, a policeman got off the bus and he said, "You're all under arrest!" Well, we were totally dumbfounded. We asked why we were being arrested, but he wouldn't tell us. The next thing we know we're on the bus. The jail was only a few blocks away. I have to admit I was scared. We got off the bus, and they gave us these numbers to hang around our necks. We were fingerprinted, and they took our pictures showing our faces and numbers. We were placed in a huge cell.

The bus left and kept picking up people and bringing them to the jail. I guess we were the first group arrested, so our cell was gradually getting filled up. There were some priests and sisters from other parishes and parishioners from Heart of Mary. And there were people from African-American communities all over Mobile—Catholics and non-Catholics. They separated the women from the men. These cell doors would open and clang, and oh, the noise! People kept arriving, I think, until the auditorium event was over. There must have been 100 or more women in our cell.

A policeman came to the cell. He seemed to know we were nuns even though we were not in the habit, and he said, "I want all the nuns to come out." We did, I don't know how many, about 20, I think. The nuns in the second car from Heart of Mary came too late and weren't arrested. The policeman said to us, "Now you've done a bad thing here." I didn't know what the bad thing was. We weren't told why we were arrested. So he kind of scolded us, then he said, "But we're going to allow you to sign yourselves out." I didn't know what we were supposed to do because I was so afraid and befuddled. Anyway, those who were thinking more clearly than I said to the policeman, "Well, if we're allowed to do this, what about the all the other women here in jail? Are you going to let them go?" He said no, no, it was just for us. So we said, "Well, we're not going to go then because we're no different than them." We didn't know what they were going to do with the other women, and we wanted to be there to witness what was happening. So we all went back into the cell. I admit I might have been a little disappointed *[She laughs.]* that we didn't get released.

A bail was placed on all of us. I don't remember what it was, but I understood you had to put up ten percent of the bail to be let go. Pretty soon black lawyers began to arrive, and they were contacting all the black businesses, particularly the biggest black businesses, the funeral homes, and getting them to put up the money. So after a few hours we did sign ourselves out, though a couple in our group—Sister Roslyn (Snyder) was one—stayed until the very end, until everybody was released.

......................................................................................

*However, the end did not come soon.* **Dora Finley** *and her mother Jocelyn Finley were also among those arrested at the auditorium. Here Dora takes over where Sister Marilyn left off.*

......................................................................................

About 13 women were still being held, and we were still in that one big cell. We were singing. The police said, "We told y'all to stop all that damn singing. We're going to take you somewhere you can sing all the damn hell you want to sing." Then they told us to take off our blouses. I remember that clearly. And our shoes too. And we said, "We'll take off our shoes. No way we're taking off our blouses." There was one lady with us who had just gotten out of the hospital. We said, "This lady over here is sick." So they said, "Come on out of there, gal." Then they took all of us out of the big cell and past this big pen, this holding cell where a lot of men were. I can remember the men sticking their hands out through the bars trying to get at us. That was scary, yeah! They took us to this place called the hole. It's a little room about the size of a bathroom. It wasn't more than eight feet high, and it had a drainage hole in the floor and some little, tiny holes at the bottom and top of the door for ventilation—like the size of a dime. There was one diamond-shaped window in the steel door. No furniture, no bathroom facilities, no sink, no nothing. All the women were put in this one place. We were cramped up. It could have been what it was like on a slave ship. We were sitting on the floor, on the cement floor surrounded by cement walls in a cramped condition, you know, just holding onto your knees. Sitting on your butt like that, it was horrible.

There was a crazy man in a cell next to us, screaming and talking about how he was going to come over and rape us. Then on the other side was this man they had arrested, who had come down here for the SCLC. He wouldn't let them fingerprint him, and they had beat him. You could hear him coughing and throwing up. He was just going, "Martin, Martin, Martin!" We would take turns going to the little holes in the door to get ventilation. Then the man from SCLC started having delusions. He said, "Oh Martin, I was with you in Selma, Martin. I was with you in Birmingham. But Martin, I ain't seen nothing like this." I will never forget what he said. We were in there for 12 hours, and it was morning when my daddy came, put up bail and got us out. One of the girls who got out had called him. Until then he didn't know we were still in jail, and he didn't know what they had done to us.

When I got out of that hole, and saw the light, my eyes started burning, and tears came to my eyes. My father said, "No, get a hold of yourself. Don't ever let them see you cry or think they can break you." *[There is a very long pause while Dora pulls herself together.]* But we left. We were safe at last. That was my first civil rights arrest; it wasn't my last.

*Another Heart of Mary grad, **Faye Johnson Malone**, got caught up in the auditorium affair without even intending to get involved.*

My mom was out of town, and my younger sisters had gone to take part in the demonstration. Someone called me and told me they were being put on a bus, being arrested. So I went downtown, and sure enough, the bus was there and they were on the bus. I went up to the policeman and I asked why my sisters were arrested. And he said, "You get on too!" As I was getting on he slapped me on my backside. And I just automatically came around and slapped him across the face. And when it ended up, I had more charges against me than the rest of them – assault and battery against a police officer. I was teaching at the time, and my principal understood the situation. She would excuse me every Friday when I had to go to court. Well, I marched after that and I was careful not to get arrested. I wasn't allowed to get arrested. I got threatened within an inch of my life. They told me, "If you're arrested again, you're not gonna go on to finish college." Eventually, they just dropped the charges.

*During her interview, **Sister Marilyn** was asked what frightened her the most about her arrest and detention at the Mobile jail.*

Well actually, my mother. *[She laughs.]* Our religious community was tremendously supportive. I wasn't afraid of our superiors. I had been raised in a very protective family. I was taught if you're in trouble, you go to the police. These are the people that will protect you. Well, I didn't feel protected in this situation. So there was a lot of disillusionment. Now my mother, she was always afraid something terrible was going to happen to me. Although there was some rioting after Martin Luther King's death, we felt protected with our parish and the African-American people. But you didn't know what was going to happen, with the police and the National Guard pointing guns at you. That was not a good feeling.

You see the thing at the auditorium was televised, and I was hoping my mother was not watching television. [She laughs.] But my family watched. They knew and then my mother knew. My mother was this very fiery Italian. You didn't want to mess with my mother. And my mother's way of handling it was to not admit it ever happened. [She laughs.] No, she never talked about it at all, never. So.... Can we change the subject please?

...................................................................................................

*The picketing and arrests continued for the remaining two days of the pageant. The city had to call out the National Guard during the event, which only helped to draw more national attention to what the black community wanted. Television cameras were everywhere, and a news helicopter hovered above the auditorium. At long last, 15 years after Rosa Parks refused to move to the back of a bus in Montgomery and six years after the Selma to Montgomery march, Mobile Alabama's call for deliverance from segregation was a national news story.*

*Giving Mobile's Catholic clergy and religious major credit, a Birmingham newspaper columnist wrote, "Without the institutional support provided by Most Pure Heart of Mary parish and the assistance of some 30 angry priests and nuns, NOW could not have been successful." Bishop Toolen apparently agreed. In a letter to the papal nuncio two days after the pageant, he said, "Most of the trouble is due to our young sisters and young priests who are agitators among the Negroes." However, he took no punitive action against them.*

*The charge against almost everyone arrested—Faye Johnson Malone being one exception—was "parading without a license." And a court date was set for the whole group. Their defense was that they were standing still when the policeman ordered them to walk back to their car. As they did so, they were stopped and put on the bus, since their act of walking was considered illegal "parading." Similar charges were brought against more than 300 people arrested during the three days of the pageant. When the accused appeared in court, they were told their hearing had been delayed until the following Friday. This delay procedure continued week after week for almost two months until all charges were finally dropped without explanation. However, many considered the cost worth the pain. After the smoke cleared, the Mobile government backed down and hired its first black assistant manger for the Municipal Auditorium.*

*Final Graduating Class, 1968*

*Sister June (Marie Jerome) Wilkerson OP with students
in HOM library in early 1960s*

# XIV. Integration: Fact or Fiction?

*The civil rights action at the Municipal Auditorium during the Junior Miss activities prompted NOW to step up pressure on many fronts. In a widely circulated "fair share" resolution with 20,000 signatures, NOW demanded an opening up of job opportunities for blacks in businesses, in city, county and state offices, in the local housing authority, in the police and sheriff's departments, and in the courts and in the schools. To press the point, NOW organized a series of marches and boycotts throughout most of 1969 and into 1970. "Operation Ghost Town" involved major boycotting of stores and businesses in downtown Mobile, and, in fact, it virtually shut down central city commerce for a time.*

*Special demonstrations were also organized to coincide with high-visibility Mobile events like the Greater Gulf States Fair and the Senior Bowl football game. The combination of these disruptions led to skirmishes and arrests, but nothing on the scale of the April auditorium crackdown. On the positive side, meetings between NOW representatives and business and government groups eventually led to concessions and pledges of progress. Meanwhile, the customs and trappings of Jim Crow that once dominated the life of the city began to disappear, not by public decree but largely by informal agreement between the Mobile establishment and the people.*

......................................................................................

**Harold DuCloux** *was amazed at the extent of the unannounced transformation.*

......................................................................................

I have some signs upstairs in my house. One says "Colored Only," and the other says "White Only." I found them in a warehouse some years ago in Plains, Geogia, President Jimmy Carter's hometown, and I got them because I realized I hadn't seen one in such a long time. I saw them as a kid growing up, of course, but it dawned on me that they disappeared overnight. They were there on Friday, and they were gone on Monday. The movement to change was subtle but effective and widespread. Mobile has a very smart business community. The businessmen said, "Look, as long as the African American community doesn't ask, we're not going to offer, but as soon as they do, we're not going to have that thing like they had in Birmingham and Montgomery. We're not going to do that. As soon as they knock on the door, we're gonna open the door, because their money is green." It may not have happened over the weekend, but it was quick, it was quick.

·····················

*The newly won benefits of desegregation notwithstanding, Heart of Mary alumni, former students and families were still in shock in 1969 due to the loss of the school. Sister Alberta (Patty Caraher) took a teaching job at the public high school in Toulminville, a Mobile suburb. It had been an all-black institution and, for practical purposes, still was all-black. SisterAntonietta (Marilyn Aiello) went to Milwaukee to teach in a Catholic school but returned to Mobile in less than a year, joining her colleague on the Toulminville faculty. Both continued living at the Heart of Mary convent. Sister Claretus (Lorraine Rivers Tucker), who took a part-time job with the NOW organization, also lived at the convent. The HOM principal, Sister Adeltrude (Roslyn Snyder), helped many former HOM staffers find new educational opportunities; she herself began teaching at Toolen, the formerly whites-only Catholic girls high school. She became the school's vice principal.*

*Many Heart of Mary alumni were in college, while others were finishing their high school education at McGill, Toolen or public schools, following the closure of Heart of Mary. In the previous chapter some expressed their feelings, mostly disappointment or anger as they grappled with change they didn't ask for. In this chapter former students look back from their perspective 45 years later. There is no unanimity here. For most, some pain and grieving is still there, even after all this time. Not just grief at the loss of their school, but sadness at the myriad ways the new era of integration they and their children and grandchildren have lived with has seemed more failure than success. For others the benefits outweigh the deficits: If integration is more ideal than reality today, there's still hope for tomorrow.*

·····················

*Carol Hill Anderson:* We knew what integration meant when we were graduating. I think we understood the reality of it. But we didn't know we were saying goodbye to history, that a chapter of history was closing.... I go to this church down the street from me now, Our Lady of Lourdes. I go mainly because it's just down the street. It's a predominantly white Catholic church, and I think they're sincere, and I'm glad I'm a Catholic. They wouldn't recruit me for anything there, you know. Every now and then I go back to Heart of Mary. They have the choir still, and the priest gives a good sermon. But it's just not the same.

*Faye Johnson Malone:* When we had desegregation, you know no whites came to black schools. We all had to go to white schools. And that took away from blacks being prepared for the outside world, having self-confidence. And that sort of thing is still going on. I went to a white church when my mom had Alzheimer's. I would go to that church because it was close and the service was fast. And the whole time I was going there I never felt a part. The white people will tell you, "Yeah, you're welcome to come to our church." They call it fellowship, but you never have the feeling of belonging. I never felt it. I just don't get anything if I have to go to Mass at the cathedral. I don't get anything out of it because I don't feel comfortable. It's supposed to be that every Catholic church is your church. But I've never felt it. And that's from back during Bishop Toolen's time.

*William Kelly:* Back then there were no tensions like we know them today in the schools. Good Lord, those were the golden years for the black community and the black youngsters in the fifties and early sixties. Those were golden years. Integration stripped us of that. I could see right away that the closing of our own schools, especially the high school, was going to be detrimental. And it has been.

*Lamar Lott:* To me integration was the worst thing that ever happened to the black schools. I have a problem with these parents today because the child can do something wrong to the teacher, and then these parents will come in, jump all over the teacher and side with the child. I raised my children different. I listened to the teacher first.

Then I got the child's side. I think the nuns would really whip the students into shape. They need Whip Wilson—Sister Wilma (Buckley). She was the one who'd walk away and slap you upside your head as she went. *[He strikes the school desk he is sitting in.]* Pow! I mean it hurt, but she got respect.

***Debra Butler:*** While schools were segregated, you were rewarded for excelling within your realm of influence. You could be the top student, you could be the student council president, you could be president of the debate team and compete with other schools. After integration none of that happened. And it's not that you were any different or any less valuable, but in a white school you just never got an award. You were never a cheerleader, you were never homecoming queen. Something really important was lost.

***Pamela Hutchinson:*** It makes me a little sad to think about it. I try to focus on the good memories and the good people. And when I look at some of our yearbooks we get out at school reunions, and I see all the names in there of those who are gone. It's like they're the people who made us who we are today—families and friends and other parents. It's sad because I feel like maybe it will never be in this world again. *[There is a long pause.]* We'll never have another Heart of Mary. It makes me sad because kids need…they need Heart of Mary in their lives. I'm sorry. I didn't mean to get so emotional.

***Lorraine Rivers Tucker (Sister Claretus):*** If I was ever angry, it was after all the work that was done to integrate the South, and then we've had years when people keep saying, "They shouldn't have any special privileges. We shouldn't make exemptions for black kids to get into college. And we shouldn't have quotas." It just felt like it was all going down the tubes. So there was a period when I was angry.

***Harold DuCloux:*** Integration killed the African-American community in Mobile. The entire black middle class moved away. You can see what Martin Luther King Avenue looks like now. When it was Davis Avenue *[named for Jefferson Davis, president of the Confederacy]*, it was the busy main street of the black population, with shops, restaurants, funeral parlors, hotels and centers for social gatherings. Now everything is gone.

*Carver Coleman:* I was kind of sad about integration, but then in a way I was glad, because the kids that would come later would go to a better school building-wise, maybe better teacher-wise too. They would get a better building block. They would socialize better. They would be better qualified *[after integration]* because there was no chance of any exploitation of Heart of Mary by whites because of the location. I just think the kids got a better education when they went to McGill-Toolen Catholic School. *[Formerly two schools, they merged in 1972.]* Now the only thing that we had that they didn't have and don't have are the nuns. The nuns were very dedicated during our time, very dedicated.

*Patricia Lofton:* Overall, I think integration was good. I had mixed emotions as I grew up. But now I think it was needed because we live in an integrated type of society. For me it was good. We learned well in our setting at Heart of Mary. But you could still do as well or better in other settings.

*Leonard Stiell:* Well, we had a close community then. When I was growing up, if I did something a block away from school, by the time I got home, my mama knew it. We used to walk back and forth to school. Kids now are being bused to schools and not necessarily in their neighborhoods. So it's hurt our neighborhoods and our relationship with people in our neighborhoods. Yes, it did open up a lot of opportunities for us. *[There is a pause.]* This is gonna sound kinda crazy. It opened up a lot of opportunities for us, but we had to give up a lot for those opportunities.

*Sheila Flanagan:* We are a desegregated community, but we're not an integrated community. And there's a big difference in that. Mobile is no different from other cities. The most segregated hour of the week is Sunday at church. There are Catholic schools and Catholic churches that come here to tour the museum, and I only see one or two black kids in the group. And some that come here I don't see any blacks at all.

I sent my son to McGill and found a lot of deficiencies there as far as how they address the topic of race and how they handle African-American students. They do a lot of tracking at McGill. If you're not a parent that fights for your child to have access, he will be put in a lower track, which lessens the possibility of him going to top-notch college. There's nobody riding the kid's back, telling him he needs to take a foreign language in order to get into a school of any value, and he needs a certain amount of math. They have conveniently let their black students go into the lower tracks. They have a few college prep courses, but few of them are actually in what they call AP (Advanced Placement).

I think it's just a sign of the times now, everywhere, everywhere – whole communities segregating themselves from Mobile because it's dominated by African-Americans. Saraland has done it. Fairhope is trying to do it. It's to keep the amount of diversity minimal. They can't get around it totally, but it's going to wind up that Mobile County will be predominantly black. You know, I have no answer for it.

But I'll tell you, I will not brood over this or live in the past. Too many people have made sacrifices to give us a choice where there used to be no choice. Unfortunately, we still have to deal with the legacy of race. I hope in your generation and my son's generation, we will make progress. It's just that people resent change. They don't normally embrace it. They're afraid of it. I don't think southerners have cornered the market on that. I think it exists everywhere.

........................................................................................................

*Is progress possible? Could the example of a remarkable place like Heart of Mary inspire creative approaches to education today? It seems most unlikely that an institution modeled on a small, segregated school of the 1950s and 1960s could contribute anything to 21st century education. In the view of several of those interviewed it would be impossible. The culture has changed. There's too much competition from the media—radio, television, Facebook, text messaging, Twitter, and the next new social media gimmick to hold the kids' attention, even with the best teachers. Besides, America is still wrestling with the legacy of race, and we're not yet enlightened enough to enable two cultures to work together,*

*Nevertheless, some individual characteristics of the education that occurred at Heart of Mary High School could be imitated, if not replicated, in the 21st century. There is no copyright, no patent on the messages that motivated several generations of students. They carried it into their later life and still marvel at it more than a half-century later. These characteristics were cited repeatedly throughout the interviews in this book. They may deserve more than passing, historical notice in the chronicles of segregated education. Here are some mentioned often and discussed by the people who lived the Heart of Mary experience.*

...........................................................................................

**Marion Lewis** *listed several lessons, though not necessarily in order of importance.*

...........................................................................................

I believe they got it right at Heart of Mary. There are lessons that can be learned and applied to other educational systems.

First, even if you have a school of 2,000 kids, you need to break it *into smaller units.* And you build communities within the school. I'm very big on that. That's part of the magic of Heart of Mary. People knew who you were. You belonged. You were part of a smaller family.

Second, the *parents must be involved* whether they want to be or not, and the teachers are involved. They know the students.

Third, there's a lot to be said for *structure* and using structure positively, not just letting kids figure out stuff on their own. Heart of Mary had structure. There was a routine to every day. I think uniforms had something to do with this too. Kids should not have to figure out what the playground is for. They should be shown. Kids really want to know what the boundaries are and told how to stay within boundaries in all aspects of school life. When you have to figure it out for yourself, that's when you have problems.

Fourth, there has to be *discipline.* Did I get my hand smacked a few times with a ruler? Yeah, sure. But it was never anything nearly as bad as people saying they were traumatized by Catholic education.

Fifth, and this is the real legacy of Heart of Mary, students need to understand and feel like they have to do something after they leave.

They *have to get involved* wherever they are, whether it's social issues or church issues. We were empowered to speak up, to take action, to make a difference. It's leadership really, and wherever you find Heart of Mary graduates, you find people who have this quality of leadership.

..................................................................................

*Other aspects of the school included resourcefulness.*

..................................................................................

**Carol Hill Anderson:** Making do with what you have is something schools can teach. We learned that in the segregated world. We were resourceful. That can work in any school system. It's sort of like this: do you know what chitlins are? That's the guts of a doggone pig. Can you imagine that's what you were given to eat? So they figured out how to survive. They figured out how to put in a little salt and pepper, throw in a little cayenne pepper. Boom-da-boom-boom! And everyone wants chitlins. So the rich folks ate the ham and all, and they gave the black folks what? The guts. Go eat this! Whew, it's deep when you think about it.

..................................................................................

*Also mentioned was an expectation of effort and achievement.*

..................................................................................

**Harold DuCloux:** What the sisters were communicating to us was, "You can do this. Here's a homework assignment in algebra or geometry or biology, and you can do this. I'm going to give you the basis to solve this equation." And so I solved the equation. I never thought about not being able to do something, not being able to solve an equation or finish a homework assignment. I never thought it was out of reach. But yeah, it was hard; it was very challenging.

**Debra Butler:** You were expected to go beyond your comfort zone. You were going to be pushed into this huge world, and you've got to be more than marginally prepared to deal with all the things that are going to happen to you.

............................................................................

*The involvement of a close-knit community was also important.*

............................................................................

***Joyce Cassino:*** What was special was the *community*. It was very *generational*. My dad graduated from Most Pure Heart of Mary, so it wasn't unusual for us to have some of the same lay instructors because they were planted there. For instance, my dad and I both had Miss Braziel. I have five siblings, so I had two sisters precede me there. Miss Brazeil knew my dad and she knew my two siblings before I attended. I had some precedents to live up to. Plus she was friends with my grandmother. They used to play bridge at the parish. So *[She laughs.]* there was a lot of oversight, a lot of reporting back to the family on what happened at school. It wasn't confining. It was normal and supportive to us. And it wasn't unusual for neighbors to call your home and say, "I saw him or her doing this after she left school," so the report was home before you even got there.

............................................................................

*Finally, a key lesson was having a dedicated teaching staff.*

............................................................................

***Cornelius Hall:*** In transferring to colleges we had an advantage that the other schools in the area did not have because of our education. We could transfer into a white school and be equal to their education because of what we got from the nuns. We were accepted. If you said, "Yeah, I went to Heart of Mary," most people would say how fortunate you are. We had science, and yeah we had good math—algebra and trigonometry and geometry. We had great labs in chemistry and biology. And in other courses like Spanish we were far ahead.

***Carver Coleman:*** The public schools thought Heart of Mary was something different, and it was, it was different. The nuns were more dedicated to teaching than the normal teacher in the public schools.

*Sister Patty Caraher's 50th jubilee celebration. Front row (left to right): Barbara Nichols Mitchell, Sister Patty, Vivian Stiell Pace. Back row: Marion Lewis, Pamela Donald Hutchinson, Leonard Stiell, Paulette Norvel Lewis.*

# XV. Great Expectations: Legacy of a School

*Though the actual initial experience of integration fell short of the expectations of its advocates, at Heart of Mary the students did not. As the voices in this book attest, the experience of an education at Most Pure Heart of Mary School had a profound affect. Why was this school so successful? How was it able to turn out so many self-assured graduates, especially in its latter years when the deep South, indeed the whole nation, was going through an era of tension and turmoil? Before reviewing the evidence—the record of what these graduates have done with their time and talent, four former members of the Heart of Mary staff provide some clues and perspective on the how and the why from their vantage point half a century later.*

.............................................................................................

*Sister Patty (Alberta) Caraher suggests that the presence of unique circumstances both in the lives of the students and in the lives of the sisters at that time and in that place served to magnify the benefits of that education.*

.............................................................................................

Our students lives were marginalized by a white society, prohibited from engaging in a world beyond their own neighborhoods where they found a close-knit society enriched by their own customs, rituals, and ways of communicating which were largely unknown by white society. The young people came to Heart of Mary High steeped in the rich background of family, neighborhood, and church. They learned early on that education was imperative if they were to engage the wider world with pride and excellence.

The sisters who staffed Heart of Mary were northerners, many of whom were near descendants of immigrants. They knew that education would make a difference in the African-American community just as it had in their own lives. They knew the meaning and experience of community, and found it deepened in their daily connection to the families and students of black Mobile whose stories found a home in their hearts. Relationships were formed and continually etched in their being.

The sisters lives were marginalized by a small black neighborhood in the days when sisters did not venture too far beyond the school, convent, and church. They had little contact with the whites of Mobile. This focus brought them into the culture of their students in a way that was unique. These aspects of the sisters lives contributed to their complete dedication to the lives they wanted to touch.

It is important then to realize that a mutual learning was taking place. How privileged we were to be brought into the deepest yearnings of the people. The intimacy we experienced at Heart of Mary was not often experienced in other educational settings. Our lives were being transformed by the people themselves and, because of them, those of us who were there during the 1950s and 1960s were able to take our cues from them and partner where we were invited. We knew that what was going to make a difference was excellence in education, and together we poured out our lives for a liberating future for the people. In so doing, we also realized that they needed consistent messages of empowering affirmation, tough love in difficult assignments, and authentic honoring of accomplishments.

..............................................................................................

*Sister Marilyn (Antonietta) Aiello notes how both positive and negative forces at work in the students' lives helped build character and provide the tools and motivation to compete in the larger world.*

..............................................................................................

There were a number of characteristics that contributed to these success stories in the lives of Heart of Mary students: tight-knit families, supportive black community, small classes, determined staff, lively faith, resourcefulness with limited supplies, and—especially—high expectations. All these worked together to provide a basis for personal stability and set a kind of foundation for life. The Heart of Mary students knew who they were, and they were happy. I think an added incentive for them was that they were treated as second class in society and, yes, in the church. It motivated them. They had the tools and they set out from that small school to disprove suppositions of their inferiority and to prove who they really were.

........................................................................................................................

*Sister Rosetta Brown offers a personal insight on the transformative effect HOM had on students. She was assigned to Heart of Mary in 1967 as a young nun. As such she was a distinct rarity in Mobile, a black sister living among whites before desegregation had really gotten off the ground. She remained at HOM for five years, teaching in the grammar school and taking classes for her degree at South Alabama University.*

........................................................................................................................

I stepped into a goldmine of sisters when I arrived at Heart of Mary. When you walked into the convent you changed. You had to. This was a special kind of community. These were a group of dreamers, and their dreams became our dreams, and our dreams became the dreams of the students. There was such respect there for one another and for every family. Those families became part of our family. You didn't hear rumors or putdowns or comments from the staff about dealing with "these little black people." No, no, they were our family. So the sisters were always attending birthday parties and weddings and funerals of the families of the students and graduates.

And the sisters had the conviction that there was nothing the students couldn't do. We had one boy who just couldn't read; everyone knew it. And Sister Nora Ryan, a reading specialist, worked so hard with him—in the library, in his house, in the convent. And when he got up at the graduation Mass and read the epistle perfectly, I can tell you there wasn't a dry eye in the house.

It's hard to explain, but you didn't hear much about Jesus or faith or belief in God in the house. These women walked the walk. They walked the Jesus walk. They believed, and they acted on what they believed. How did this happen for so many years? I really think you can trace it back to Sister Martin De Porres Hogan, *[the first high school principal when the Sinsinawa Dominicans came to Mobile in 1943]*. I think she set a tone when she came. And the sisters picked up on it. I don't think any of our sisters were ever the same after Mobile. I know I wasn't.

........................................................

*Father John Harfmann, who threw himself into the school and its activities in the mid-1960s, stressed his conviction that there were lessons learned here that deserve to be replicated today, but in a different century and a much changed cultural setting.*

........................................................

The story of what began as a process has to be told and told over and over again because young people today would not have any idea what this history is all about. Heart of Mary opened a future to many who didn't even think there was a future. You have to keep retelling the story and seeing the tough days and the glory days and what happened to them after. But it would have to be created in a new way and at a new time and under new circumstances. But it has to be done.

*Here are brief bios of some of those who were interviewed for this book. Most are former HMO students but also included are some faculty and staff members. All are listed alphabetically by their first names, since in many cases, maiden names were changed at the time of marriage.*

**ALEXIS HERMAN**, the first black person to serve as U.S. Secretary of Labor, was a 1965 HOM graduate and has held many positions in government and business during her career. After her graduation from Xavier University, majoring in sociology, she worked for Catholic Charities, advocating for minority women employment. In 1976 she was co-chair of the National Call to Action Conference in Detroit, sponsored by the U.S. Catholic bishops in an effort to implement the Second Vatican Council. The next year, President Jimmy Carter named her director of the U.S. Labor Department's Women's Bureau; at 29 she was the youngest person to serve in that post. She then became chief of staff of the Democratic National Committee and later the committee's vice chair. In the latter post, she was responsible for organizing the 1992 Democratic National Convention. After Bill Clinton's presidential victory in 1992, she served as deputy director of the Presidential Transition Office. She was then appointed head of the White House Office of Public Liaison. During Clinton's second term, she was appointed his Secretary of Labor, though her nomination was much opposed by the Republicans in Congress. During the 2000 Florida election recount, she was part of the team planning the transition to an Al Gore presidency and considered a top candidate for White House Chief of Staff. She founded her own consulting firm in 1981 and is a board member of several major companies, including Coca-Cola, Toyota, and Metro Goldwyn Mayer. She is a member of the HOM Hall of Fame.

**AURELIA "BOOTSIE" TAYLOR CHES-TANG,** a 1957 HOM graduate, studied fashion design for two and a half years at a Brooklyn, New York, design school. She then studied social work at the University of Chicago and later served as the dean of social work at the University of Detroit. She lived in Chicago for a time where she became a political activist. Most of her contribution to the world of fashion, she said, has been through the clothes she's made for her two daughters. She is a sister of Autherine Taylor.

**AUTHERINE TAYLOR** graduated from HOM in 1948, then studied at Howard University in Washington, D.C., for three years, continued her studies at Mexico City College in Mexico, and eventually earned a degree in counseling at Columbia Teachers College in New York City. She then served as a dorm director at Howard University. She also taught at a Patterson, New Jersey, elementary school before taking a position as a librarian at South Alabama University. Now retired, she is a sister of Aurelia Taylor Chestang.

**CAROL HILL ANDERSON,** who graduated from HOM in 1968, earned a bachelor's degree in economics at Mundelein College in Chicago and worked for a time as an affirmative action officer for Bradenton County, Florida. She then served as chief of compliance for the city of St. Petersburg, Florida. Returning to Mobile, she worked as an administrative assistant in the Mobile County office of CETA (Comprehensive Employment and Education Training Act) and in the same capacity for the county license commissioner's office, while raising her two children and assisting in raising her three nieces. She also was a real estate salesperson for some years. Later, she attended Loyola University in New Orleans, where she received her law degree. She is now a practicing attorney in the Mobile area.

**CARVER COLEMAN** attended Xavier University in New Orleans after graduating from Heart of Mary. He received a degree in pharmacy and worked as a pharmacist in Mobile for 40 years. He established his own pharmacy in 1973, maintaining it until his retirement in 1988. He and his wife have been married for 43 years and have a daughter and a grandson.

**CLARETTA DANIELS** graduated from Heart of Mary in 1942 and majored in home economics at Xavier University. She taught kindergarten at Heart of Mary for three years and in the lower grades at the school for another 23 years. When the Head Start program was introduced to Mobile in the 1960s, she served as a counselor. She has children and grandchildren in the Mobile area.

**CORNELIUS HALL,** a 1956 HOM graduate who passed away in 2012, attended Tuskegee Institute for three years before joining the U.S. Navy and moving to San Francisco. He joined the Alameda, California, Fire Department and became the first black lieutenant in that department. During his tenure with the Alameda firefighters, he worked with activist groups to open job opportunities for minorities. In retirement he was a member of the HOM alumni board and a volunteer at the school. He was married for many years to Patricia Hardwick.

**DEBRA BUTLER** has had an extensive education and a wide-ranging career since her HOM graduation in 1968. She obtained a bachelor's degree in arts from the University of Miami, a master's in education

from Harvard University and a master's in business administration from Spring Hill College in Mobile. In addition she earned a certificate from the Kennedy School of Government at Harvard. She is currently working on a master's degree from the International Business School at Brandeis University in Boston and on a doctorate from the Heller School for Social Policy and Management, also at Brandeis. Meanwhile, she has been program coordinator for the external degree program at Florida International University, program coordinator/instructor at Faulkner State Community College in Alabama, and executive director of Leadership Mobile, assisting managers in business and education. She had a lengthy career with Delta and Swissair airlines as training and management coordinator for international flight attendant crews. She has also been a financial advisor for Morgan Stanley/Merill Lynch regarding risk management, investment, and business valuation. Recently she served as a research intern at the World Economic Forum in New York City. She is a member of the Heart of Mary Hall of Fame. Her daughter is a student at Princeton University.

**DORA FINLEY** attended Heart of Mary from kindergarten through her second year of high school, then voluntarily enrolled at Toolen High School to support the call for integration. At Toolen she organized the Student Action Movement, which supported the few black students there, dealt with inter-racial problems, and served as a kind of negotiating board to settle disputes. She graduated from Toolen in 1969. Her grandfather, James Franklin,

was the first black physician in Mobile, and her father, James Finley, was a well-known pharmacist and activist for civil rights in the city.

She earned a degree from Eastern Michigan University and began a 25-year career as logistics manager for Scott Paper Co./Kimberly Clark Corp. She was an extremely active organizer of community foundations, including the Alabama Trust for Historic Preservation, the Historic Mobile Preservation Society, and the Jewish-Christian Dialogue. Her major legacy was as president and driving force behind the African-American Heritage Trail, which has so far erected more than 40 markers throughout Mobile in recognition of African-American people, places, and events. She had one daughter, a large extended family, and scores of friends and admirers who grieved her passing in 2012.

**ELAINE PALMER** is a 1941 HOM graduate who went to Alabama A&M University for one year. She was married in 1946 and moved to New York City. Disliking the cold weather, the growing family returned to Mobile. Elaine had nine children, five girls and four boys, all of whom graduated from Heart of Mary High School, except the youngest two, who graduated from Toolen after HOM closed in 1968.

**GARY COOPER** graduated from Notre Dame University with a degree in finance. He joined the Marine Corps, and during his career as a Marine rose to the rank of major general, the second black person to reach that level. He was the first black Marine officer to lead an infantry company into battle and was wounded twice during the Vietnam War. He has held a variety of significant positions since his return to civilian life: appointed U.S. ambassador to Jamaica, elected to a seat in the Alabama legislature, served on the cabinet of Alabama Gov. George Wallace, appointed head of the Alabama Department of Human Resources, and named assistant secretary of the U.S. Air Force. Cooper was one of the founders of Commonwealth National Bank in Mobile, one of the few black-owned banks in the country. He holds an honorary doctorate from Troy University, still serves on national boards, and is much involved in charitable, civil rights, and church activities in Mobile. He is married and has three children. Like him, a son and grandson are also graduates of Notre Dame. He is a member of the HOM Hall of Fame.

**SISTER GENEVIEVE SOGOTA OCD** graduated from Heart of Mary High School in 1950 and six months later joined the Discalced Carmelite religious order at their house in Mobile. She was the cook for the community for more than 50 years and, as a Carmelite, could leave the premises only for a short time and with special permission. A group of younger Carmelite sisters from Vietnam has since moved into the Carmelite monastery, so she and her fellow retired religious have settled in the Sisters of Mercy convent in Mobile while the Vietnamese nuns remodel the Carmelite house.

**HAROLD DU CLOUX** enrolled at Tuskegee Institute after graduating from Heart of Mary in 1966. He earned there the degree of doctor of veterinary medicine. He then entered South Alabama University Medical School and graduated in 1978 with a degree of doctor of medicine (MD), specializing in family practice. (He and Sister Marilyn Aiello took a number of classes together at South Alabama.) Harold then served in the U.S. Army as a doctor with posts in eight different army installations, ranging from Texas to Korea, over the next 22 years. After resigning from the military, he and his wife moved to Milwaukee, Wisconsin, where he is currently in urgent care practice. He and his wife, Joyce Cassino, have two children.

**JACQUELINE RICE** worked for a Mobile photographer after graduating from HOM in 1941, then moved to Chicago to care for her ailing sister who was living there. She moved to Philadelphia, got

married, had a daughter, moved back to Chicago, and finally returned to Mobile in 1951, where she has lived since. She has one daughter, Pamela Donald Hutchinson.

**FATHER JOHN GEORGE HARFMANN SSJ**, was a priest of the Josephite order whose first assignment was to St. Peter Claver Church in Baltimore. He was then transferred to Heart of Mary as a religion teacher in the school and associate to the pastor. Afterwards, he moved around the country: to Baltimore to direct the urban church office, to Washington, D.C. to staff the Josephite pastoral center, back to Baltimore, to Houston, and to Los Angeles as director of the archdiocesan center for evangelization. He was then elected to the post of consultant general for the entire Josephite community. His last position before his death in 2013 was as pastor of Corpus Christi-Epiphany Church in New Orleans.

**JOYCE CASSINO**, a 1967 HOM graduate, attended Cameron University in Oklahoma, earning a bachelor's degree in education. She later got a master's degree in social work at Savannah State University. While accompanying her husband, Dr. Harold DuCloux, on his assignments to various army bases, she worked in early childhood education on the same bases as a teacher, curriculum specialist, and in other capacities. Since moving to Milwaukee after her husband of 45 years resigned from the army, she has been a volunteer social worker at the local veterans hospital. They have two children, a daughter who is a YMCA executive and a son who is a federal public defender in Portland, Oregon.

**LAMAR LOTT** graduated from HOM in 1962 and served as a U.S. Army combat soldier during the Vietnam War. He moved to California, near Los Angeles, and became a truck driver for USF Holland freight services, working there some 30 years. He then returned to Mobile to help care for his aging mother and continued as a driver for Holland in Alabama. He is a member of the Lott family, known for their loyalty to Heart of Mary School. Now retired, Lamar is married and has four children. One of  the revered members of the Lott family is his father, Clarence Lott, Jr., class of 1932. He had seven children, four of whom attended HOM. As of the publication of this book, Clarence is the oldest living graduate of the high school.

**LARLEITTA CROCKETT HALL**, a 1944 HOM graduate, earned a bachelor's degree, majoring in home economics with a minor in English, at Tuskegee Institute. She taught taught home economics and English at Williamson High School in Mobile for 35 years. Widowed at an early age, she has one daughter, Debra Butler.

**LEONARD STIELL** joined the Air Force after graduation from HOM in 1968. When he returned to civilian life, he went to work for AT&T, first in Alexandria, Louisiana, then in Mobile. For 35 years he remained with the company, first as a linesman, then in installation, finally in cable splicing. He and his wife, Linda, have been married 39 years and have three children and four grandsons. Well known for his willingness to take on hard tasks, Stiell, now retired, is very active in his parish and in support of Heart of Mary Elementary School.

SISTER MARILYN AIELLO OP (formerly Sister Antonietta), a Chicago native, entered the Sinsinawa Dominican religious order after high school and taught at HOM for four years before being assigned to an integrated school in Washington, D.C., where she became involved in hosting the Poor People's March in 1968. After a brief assignment in Milwaukee, she returned to Mobile and began teaching at Toulminville High School. She took time to finish her master's degree at Southern Methodist

University in Dallas. Then she went to South Alabama University to obtain a doctor of medicine degree and followed up with her residency in family medicine in the Chicago area. Thus began her work helping establish medical clinics in doctor-scarce areas. She was instrumental in launching the Franklin clinics in Mobile. With other sisters, she founded a health center in Marks, Mississippi, and a clinic in Lexington, Mississippi. During these ventures, she taught and saw patients in the family medicine department at the University of Mississippi Medical Center in Jackson. Now technically retired, she is the medical consultant for her Dominican order and a member of the HOM Hall of Fame.

MARION LEWIS attended South Alabama University and the University of Cincinnati after graduation. He was hired by the Burger Chef restaurant chain, becoming their youngest restaurant manager ever at the age of 19 and gradually moving up to supervisor of management development. He then moved to Pizza Hut as personnel and training manger for the Midwest, overseeing 140 stores. He later became a franchise owner of seventeen Pizza Hut and Boston Market locations in

the Atlanta area. The next step was to Wendy's restaurants as director of training for the entire southeast region. He took early retirement but soon launched his own executive training, coaching and consulting firm. He also writes customized training programs for businesses and is an active Catholic with his parish council, youth choir, and liturgy training. He is married to Paulette Norvel Lewis.

**MILTON JOYNER** attended the University of Philadelphia and South Alabama University after graduation, majoring in advertising and marketing. He worked for a time with the Internal Revenue Service in Philadelphia, then returned to Mobile, establishing his own advertising firm. He worked closely for many years on behalf of local political candidates, including Michael Figures, the first black state senator in Alabama, Mobile Mayor Sam Jones, and various county commissioners. He had his own Mobile clothing store, M.J. Fashions, for 12 years. Now retired, he has two daughters and a grandson.

**PAMELA DONALD HUTCHINSON,** who graduated in the last HOM high school class in 1968, obtained a degree in business management at Alabama A&M University. She moved to Baton Rouge, Louisiana, and took a position as executive assistant to then Louisiana State Treasurer Mary Landrieu. She then became executive assistant to the Louisiana lieutenant governor. Her next post was deputy secretary to the director of the state's Department of Revenue. She concluded her governmental career as deputy secretary for the director of the Louisiana Department of Social Services. She and her husband have one daughter.

**SISTER PATRICIA "PATTY" CARAHER OP,** (formerly Sister Alberta) grew up in Chicago, where she attended the same high school as Sister Marilyn Aiello. She entered the Sinsinawa Dominicans after two years of college and first taught at Our Lady of Refuge School in the Bronx, New York. She was then assigned to Heart of Mary in 1960. When the high school closed in 1968, she was hired at Toulminville High School to teach English and work as a guidance counselor. While there, she was involved in student and faculty protests promoting the integration of schools. She later started Link, a program to connect local residents with their family members in prison. In 1975, she moved to Chicago's Uptown neighborhood, where she worked with Friendship  House and helped found a not-for-profit day labor agency. Later, while ministering in Fort Meyers, Florida, she helped establish a social service agency and a migrant camp tutoring program. She then served on the Sinsinawa Dominican Southern Province leadership team for ten years. Her most recent endeavor was to co-found the International Community School in Atlanta, Georgia, a free charter elementary school whose mission is to serve children refugees of war alongside locally born children. In 2012, she was presented the Lewis Hine Award by the National Child Labor Committee for her lifetime work and advocacy on behalf of children.

**PATRICIA LEWIS HARDWICK** graduated from high school in 1966 and attended Tuskegee Institute, obtaining a bachelor's degree in art and fashion design. She also earned three master's degrees in special education administration and supervision from Alabama State University. In addition, she took courses at Auburn University and taught for 33 years in Mobile County high schools. She was the recipient of numerous awards and honors during her teaching career. She is the widow of Cornelius Hall.

**PATRICIA KELLY LOFTON** attended Heart of Mary from first grade until the school closed in 1968. After graduating from Toolen, she went to South Alabama University, earning bachelor's and master's degrees in elementary education and an AA certification in educational administration, supervision, and elementary education. During her 30-year career in education, she served at several Mobile schools, including Barton and Craighead, as teacher, resource teacher, supervisor, and director of the staff development center. Since retirement, she has been an adjunct teacher at Bishop State Community College and hosts seminars in child care training. She has two children and one grandchild. She is a sister of William Kelly.

**PAULETTE NORVEL LEWIS** entered the Sinsinawa Dominican religious order after graduation from high school. She attended Edgewood College in Madison, Wisconsin, earning a bachelor's degree in education and a double minor in sociology and theology. She left the order after five years and began working in New York with the Recruitment and Training Program (RTP), a minority placement organization where she became co-founder (with Alexis Herman) and director of the Women's Employment Division. She then moved to the U.S. Small Business Administration as a regional administrator. In the 1980s, she served as chief of employment development for the City of Atlanta, then moved to the Martin Luther King Center as chief of staff for Coretta Scott King. Later she worked as a regional marketing manager for a civil engineering firm. In 2006, she was hired as regional administrator for the U.S. Department of Labor Women's Bureau. She is co-author of the book *Moving Up: Placing Minority Women in Management Positions*. She is married to Marion Lewis.

**SHEILA FLANAGAN** has been assistant director of the Museum of Mobile for more than 15 years. She attended Heart of Mary High School for two years before transferring to Toolen High when desegregation of schools became mandatory. After graduation, she earned a bachelor's degree in political science and history at Southern University in Baton Rouge, Louisiana. She then earned a master's degree in public administration at South Alabama University. She worked closely with Dora Finley in creating the African-American Heritage Trail in Mobile and is a member of the trail committee. She has one son, a student at William & Mary University.

**FATHER WILLIAM JAMES**, a priest of the Mobile Archdiocese, was assistant superintendent of Catholic Schools and an official in the church's chancery office in the 1950s and early 1960s. He became pastor of St. Francis Xavier Church in Toulminville, where he encouraged civil rights activity and opened the church to civil rights advocates. He then served as pastor at City of St. Jude, a unique parish, school and social service center for handicapped children in Montgomery, Alabama. Before retirement, he pastored churches in Phenix City and Robertsdale, Alabama.

**WILLIAM KELLY**, a 1956 HOM graduate, was hired as a janitor at the Mobile Sears store and worked his way up to head janitor. Moved by an urge to strive higher, he began taking courses at Spring Hill College. He eventually earned a bachelor's degree in the humanities and launched a career as a religion teacher and football coach, first at McGill High School, then at a high school in New Orleans, then back at the combined McGill-Toolen High School. He is a brother of Patricia Kelly Lofton.

*Space or time limitations prevented the inclusion of testimony by other Heart of Mary supporters who might have added their testimony and stories about this amazing institution. Here are short bios of a few of them.*

**BILL "BUTCH" HOLMES**, a 1963 HOM graduate, earned a bachelor's degree in accounting and business from Xavier University, a master's in business administration from Roosevelt University in Chicago, and a certification in eliminating waste from the University of Kentucky. He had a 38-year career at Rexam Beverage Cans Company (formerly National Cans Company). He then held a variety of positions with U.S. Cellular, including plant controller, plant manager and director of manufacturing for North and South America. He has also been a consultant with Blue Cross-Blue Shield and British Petroleum. Since retirement, he has done volunteer spiritual work with several Chicago area hospitals and at the Cook County Jail. He is a mentor for Big Brothers/Big Sisters and was named Big Brother of the year in Chicago in 2010. He and his wife Janis have one child and two grandchildren.

**JENNIFER JOHNSON HENDERSON** was among the first Heart of Mary students to voluntarily switch to Toolen High School in 1963 in the interest of desegregation. After graduation she majored in pharmacy at Xavier University, then became chief lab assistant to a doctor at South Alabama University Medical School who was doing experimental work seeking to aid children with endocrine disorders. She spent a year at the University of Arkansas developing her lab skills in this field with Dr. Jocelyn Elders, who later became U.S. surgeon general under President Bill Clinton. She returned to her work at South Alabama, then took a job with Curtin Matheson Scientific, selling medical supplies to hospitals and doctors in three states. Next, she and her husband purchased the Vincent Restaurant in Birmingham and managed it for several years. Her abiding interest for the past 24 years has been selling insurance; she is now with Mutual Savings Life Insurance. She has one son.

**JOSEPH BELL**, a 1963 HOM graduate, attended Alabama State University (where he was an outstanding football player), earning a bachelor's degree in health and physical education. He earned a master's degree in education at Howard University. He worked as a football coach at high schools in Alabama, Minneapolis, and St. Paul, Minnesota (the first black person to hold that position in St. Paul), and as baseball coach and assistant football coach at Hampton Institute in Virginia. He then launched a 40-year career as director of three programs at Howard University to assist low-income high school youth to prepare for college and aiding low-income students already in college. At Howard he was also swimming coach and assistant football coach. Before retirement, he was interim athletic director at Howard. In retirement he is a deacon in the Archdiocese of Washington and chaplain of the Newman Club at Howard University. He and his wife have two children.

**MELVIN WASHINGTON**, a 1964 HOM graduate, has a bachelor's degree in electrical engineering from Howard University and a master's in business administration from New York University. He also completed the administration executive education program at the Wharton School of Business at the University of Pennsylvania. During his financial career he held executive level positions at several major firms, including AT&T, Solomon Brothers, Morgan Stanley, and Citibank. In 2002,  he shifted to the non-profit field as chief operating officer at Human Rights First and at the East-West Institute, and as chief executive officer of a micro-lending company. Now retired in Mobile, he remains on the boards of several New York charitable and health organizations and is an active cyclist and runner, with some 30 marathons under his belt.

**SHEILA WILSON WHITE** graduated in 1963 from Heart of Mary and earned a degree in education and library science at Alabama State University. She taught at the Craighead/George Hall Elementary School for some 30 years, retiring in 2002. For many years she served with the Drug Education Council in Mobile and continues as a drug prevention specialist, working with teachers and students in the schools of Mobile County. She and her husband have two children and four grandchildren.

**SANDRA PARKER LEATHERWOOD** is a Sinsinawa Dominican Associate and the Director of Schools in the Diocese of Charleston, South Carolina. Her mother graduated from HOM and taught in the grade school there. Several of her siblings also attended HOM.

# Acknowledgments

**ROBERT MCCLORY** is a professor emeritus at Northwestern University's Medill School of Journalism and is a former reporter and editor for the Chicago Defender. His articles have appeared in numerous magazines, and he is a long-time writer for the *National Catholic Reporter.* He is the author of eight books including *Faithful Dissenters: Men and Women Who Loved and Changed the Church.*

I would like to thank the many people who are responsible for the creation of this book. It was a team effort from the beginning. First and foremost is the original committee that conceived the project, Sinsinawa Dominican Sisters Patricia "Patty" Caraher and Marilyn Aiello, Alexis Herman, and Paulette Norvel Lewis. They believed an account of Most Pure Heart of Mary School, based on the actual voices of those who attended it, would make a valuable contribution to our understanding of the interface of race, religion, education, and authority as the era of civil rights was arriving in the deepest South. It was true of course that those who could speak from experience were 40 to 50 years removed from their days at Heart of Mary, and memory is a fragile faculty at best. But Sisters Patty and Marilyn found several dozen who were eager to cooperate. In addition to former students, some former faculty and others connected with the school were interviewed to help provide context. Those who participated also provided basic information on their lives and careers after leaving Heart of Mary, giving a graphic picture of the profound impact Heart of Mary has had on their lives.

Foremost among the interviewers was Karen Skalitzky, who personally conducted more than 20 in-depth interviews. Among the transcribers were Kate Hennessy, granddaughter of Dorothy Day, founder of the Catholic Worker movement and Johannah Turner, whose godparents were Dorothy Day and Peter Maurin. Others who worked diligently on the interview team were Paul Ferguson and students from Spring Hill College: Jacob Browning, Hannah Zimmerman, Mark Brink, and Daniel Cassanova, all students of Dr. Thomas Ward Jr., whose course on oral history focused on Heart of Mary High School.

Much appreciated are those who helped finance the project. They include the John C. and Carolyn Noonan Parmer Private Foundation, the Sinsinawa Dominicans, the Honorable Alexis Herman, the Aiello family, the Josephite Fathers, Paulette and Marion Lewis, and the National Center for the Laity.

I wish to thank those who went out of their way to assist me in putting all this together. They include Leonard Stiell, Pam Donald Hutchinson, Paulette Norvel Lewis, Sister Lois Hoh OP, Bill "Butch" Holmes, all the interviewees who gave of their time, and especially, those who provided photos of themselves. My wife Margaret and our daughter, Jennifer, and her partner, Sarah Klein, provided encouragement, critical comment, and a watchful eye on this project, for which I am most grateful. I also thank Joe Fitzharris for his creative suggestions.

Gregory Pierce, president of ACTA Publications, deserves much gratitude for his interest in the idea and his willingness to take on the project. Greg's associate, Patricia Lynch, of Harvest Graphics, deserves special recognition for her design and typesetting of the book.

Finally, it should be noted that the tapes and transcriptions used in this book are archived at the Sinsinawa Dominican Motherhouse and the University of South Alabama, where they will be made available for any scholarly and educational purposed deemed appropriate by the archivists. All profits from the sale of this book will go to the education of African American students, with priority to the Tuition Assistance Fund for students who attend most Pure Heart of Mary Elementary School. If Most Pure Heart of Mary Elementary School should ever close, these profits will be used for tuition assistance for African American students of other Sinsinawa Dominican schools.

# Index